T0356384

The Virginia House-wife

Mary Randolph by Saint-Mémin.
Courtesy of the Virginia State Library

The Virginia House-wife

200th Anniversary Edition

Mary Randolph

A facsimile of the first edition, 1824, along
with additional material from the editions
of 1825 and 1828, thus presenting a
complete text.

Historical commentary by
Karen Hess

Foreword by
Debra Freeman

THE UNIVERSITY OF
SOUTH CAROLINA PRESS

Published by the University of South Carolina Press
Columbia, South Carolina 29208

uscpress.com

Printed in the United States of America

Library of Congress Cataloging-in-Publication
Data can be found at http://catalog.loc.gov/.

ISBN: 978-1-64336-551-0 (hardcover)

Facsimile reproductions of the 1824 edition of this
work and the plates and explanation in the 1825
edition were obtained from copies in the collection
of the American Antiquarian Society, Worcester,
Massachusetts, whose cooperation the publisher
most gratefully acknowledges.

Contents

Foreword

by Debra Freeman

The Virginia House-wife by Mary Randolph was a cookbook sensation when it was published in 1824. In the 1984 edition of the book, culinary historian Karen Hess's introduction provides a crucial historical backdrop that outlines not only why this text was significant for its time but also the enormous contributions of enslaved cooks. In contrast, Randolph's only mention of enslaved people was in her introduction where she noted, "We have no right to expect slaves or hired servants to be more attentive to our interest than we ourselves are."

Randolph's book was heralded as the first regional American cookbook and was so popular that it was reprinted at least nineteen times by the start of the Civil War. That the quote above was the only mention of the enslaved people who were forced to labor for her has meant that their material and creative contributions were effectively hidden from generations of readers. Yet it is not difficult to imagine that many of the recipes listed draw inspiration, if not direct instruction, from the enslaved people who were toiling in the kitchen from dusk until dawn each day. Perhaps the most notable enslaved chef that Randolph would have had contact with was James Hemings, who was the property of Thomas Jefferson at Monticello. Randolph's brother, Thomas Randolph Mann, was Jefferson's son-in-law, and historical evidence supports that the families spent significant time together in Charlottesville. In addition, after the death of Jefferson's wife, Randolph became the hostess of Monticello and daily served the half-Virginian and half-French that Hemings and others in Jefferson's kitchen crafted. Because of this, Randolph had firsthand knowledge of and proximity to how meals were prepared.

Hess's introduction also nods to the French influences in the text, and she writes that "Possible sources are legion." One likely source was Hemings. Hemings was born enslaved in 1765, and when Jefferson was appointed as ambassador to France in 1784, he took Hemings to Paris for the sole purpose of him learning how to cook the French food that Jefferson enjoyed.

For two years Hemings studied under some of the best chefs in France, and he returned to America with new recipes and techniques that show up in Randolph's book.

One of the recipes in the cookbook that most clearly appears to borrow heavily from Hemings's French training is the recipe for macarons (which she spells "macaroone"). It describes how to make the delicate treat: "whip the whites of seven eggs to a strong froth, put in one pound of powdered sugar, beat it some time, then put in the almonds." According to one of the most respected culinary schools in the world, Le Cordon Bleu, in the French method of making macarons, egg whites are whisked until a stiff-peaked meringue forms. From there, powdered sugar and ground almonds are folded in slowly. It is rather unlikely that Randolph, who was not trained in French technique, would independently be able to come up with the exact proper method to make what is arguably one of the most challenging French desserts. However, Hemings's French training would have given him the knowledge and technique needed to make such an intricate dessert.

It should be noted that other cooks at Monticello were also responsible for Jefferson's dinners being noted as half-Virginian and half-French, including James Hemings's brother

Peter, whom James trained to take his place once he was granted his freedom from Jefferson, and who became the head chef from 1796 to 1809. Edith Hern Fossett later replaced Peter as head cook and helmed the kitchen from 1809 to 1826. Fossett had previously worked in the White House kitchen along with Frances Hern and Ursula Granger Hughes; altogether they worked for nearly two decades in the Monticello kitchen after Jefferson was no longer president.

The Virginia House-wife is an incredible snapshot of dining and Southern life before the Civil War, and as a historical text, it is an invaluable tool. However, when reading the text, we must keep in mind that it was enslaved men and women who labored and had to possess the skill, creativity, and intelligence needed to ensure that these dishes were served at the highest level for their enslavers. The enslaved men and women created dishes that endure hundreds of years later, and it is imperative to recognize the culinary legacy they left behind.

Virginia, 2024

Acknowledgments

I want to express my deep appreciation to the editors at University of South Carolina Press for their work in restoring to the American people the unjustly neglected work of Mary Randolph, our First Lady of American cookery. It is part of our national heritage. I am touched by the editors' having entrusted this Yankee with *The Virginia House-wife,* and I am grateful for the opportunity of having been able to continue my work on the history of American cookery.

And I want to express my continuing appreciation of my friend Elizabeth David, a font of knowledge and source of inspiration to those of us who write about food. Among other things, it was she who taught me the worth of English cookery and the importance of going back to the roots of one's own cookery. I also want to acknowledge my indebtedness to the late Eleanor Lowenstein, bibliographer, who was so patient with me when I first started digging into early American cookbooks.

Among the libraries who graciously extended special courtesies to me, I want to name the American Antiquarian Society of Worcester, the Rare Book Collections of the New York Public Library, and the Alderman Library of the University of Virginia. In addition, I want to thank Frank Anderson, Rudolf Grewe, Betty Morefield, and Barbara Scott, for elucidating minor points. And my husband John for putting up with it all.

KAREN HESS
New York, 1983

Historical Notes and Commentaries on Mary Randolph's *The Virginia House-wife*

by Karen Hess

The most influential American cookbook of the nineteenth century was *The Virginia House-wife* by Mary Randolph (1824). There are those who regard it as the finest book ever to have come out of the American kitchen, and a case may be made for considering it to be the earliest full-blown American cookbook. Mrs. Randolph's heyday was in the 1790's, so that her work may be said to document the cookery of the early days of our republic. It was one of the most cherished of kitchen manuals; Virginia Randolph Trist's copy of the manuscript collection of recipes kept by Martha Jefferson Randolph, for example, contains over fifty recipes from the book, all painstakingly copied and individually attributed to "Mrs. Mary Randolph." Yet, few writers today have bothered to study the work, as witnessed by the arrant nonsense written in our most respected journals on early culinary practice, particularly in regard to the use of tomatoes and other vegetables. Even those who cite the work have an unfortunate tendency to place its publication in 1860, and so obfuscate its historical importance. But before attempting to assess this importance, let us pause for a moment to find out who Mary Randolph was.

In 1929, during the restoration of Arlington House,[1] workers found the grave of one "Mrs. Mary Randolph" not far from the mansion. According to the gravestone, she had been born on August 9, 1762, "at Amptill near Richmond, Virginia," and died January 23, 1828, "in Washington City." Her epitaph states that "her intrinsic worth needs no eulogium," but she had been sadly forgotten. According to Margaret Husted,[2] it was only after an article about the

[1]It was built by George Washington Parke Custis, beginning 1802, and became the residence of Robert E. Lee after his marriage to Mary Anne Randolph Custis. The adjoining Arlington Cemetery lies on former Custis lands.

[2]*Virginia Cavalcade*, Vol. XXX, No. 2, 1980. Indeed, I wish to acknowledge my debt to the late Mrs. Husted for the unearthing of certain facts used in these brief biographical notes.

unknown lady appeared in *The Washington Star* that her descendants came forward to supply information about her and her work. She was, of course, our Mary Randolph, author of *The Virginia House-wife*.

Mary Randolph was the daughter of Anne Cary Randolph and Thomas Mann Randolph of Tuckahoe, in Goochland County. In 1782, she married David Meade Randolph, and in the years that followed they made Moldavia, their imposing home in Richmond, celebrated for their displays of "lavish hospitality."

In 1802, however, David Randolph, "a bitterly outspoken federalist," was removed from the comfortable appointive office of United States marshal by Thomas Jefferson and the financial fortunes of the Randolphs never again prospered. By 1808, in spite of having given up Moldavia, these embarrassments became acute and Mrs. Randolph advertised in the March 4 issue of *The Richmond Virginia Gazette and General Advertiser* that she was opening a boardinghouse. By all accounts, the food and accommodations were splendid, even if one dismisses some tales as apocryphal.

Late in 1819, according to Mrs. Husted, the Randolphs moved to Washington, where Mrs. Randolph took up the work of committing to paper her long culinary experience for what was to be *The Virginia House-wife*.

Social relationships and ties of blood among the first families of Virginia were endlessly convoluted. According to Mrs. Husted, Mary was the cousin of G. W. P. Custis and is thought to have been the godmother of his daughter Mary Anne Randolph Custis.

Now, Custis was the grandson of Martha Dandridge Washington by her first husband, Daniel Custis, through whose family the Washington MS. had passed. This manuscript was bequeathed by Martha to Nelly Custis Lewis, her granddaughter, so that it is not impossible that Mary Randolph knew the work.

And according to Edwin Morris Betts,[3] the family of Thomas Jefferson spent the early years of his childhood in Tuckahoe as neighbors and friends of the Randolphs. Thomas Mann Randolph, Jr., Mary's younger brother, married Jefferson's daughter Martha in 1790 at Monticello. This Randolph was a farmer, member of Congress, and Governor of Virginia. (Also, see Harriet Randolph Hackley.)

So it can be seen that, in addition to her culinary prowess, nobody was more qualified by reason of family and social milieu to record the cookery of Virginia, the home of so many of our founding fathers, and of our nation's capital as well, in those early days.

[3]*Thomas Jefferson's Garden Book, 1766–1824*, edited by Edwin Morris Betts. All gardening information attributed to Jefferson comes from this source.

In order to better understand the place of *The Virginia House-wife* in American culinary history, it is necessary to examine for a moment the cookbooks that Americans had previously been using.

The early colonists brought with them their most trusted cookbooks, first among them being family manuscript collections, a certain number of which survive. Among them is one which eventually came to be in the possession of Martha Washington, which is of particular interest to us here because of its Virginia associations. The recipes date from Elizabethan and Jacobean times although the copying may have taken place in mid-seventeenth century, possibly in preparation for emigration to Virginia. One cannot understand American cookery without some knowledge of the mother cuisine, that of sixteenth- and seventeenth-century England, and these family manuscripts are the purest source because they represent actual practice down through the generations rather than what some professional cook or editor deemed proper.

A number of printed cookbooks were early brought to these shores as well. Mary Tolford Wilson[4] writes that records of the Virginia Company show that by 1620, copies of Gervase

[4]Amelia Simmons, *American Cookery* (1796), in facsimile. Introduction by Mary Tolford Wilson. Oxford University Press, 1958.

Markham's *The English Huswife* (1615) and *The English Husbandman,* "bound together," were readied for shipment to America. Using eighteenth-century inventories and sales records, Jane Carson[5] gives a list of cookbooks to be found in Virginia homes, the most popular of which was *The Art of Cookery* by Hannah Glasse (London, 1747). It went through innumerable editions and revisions and was easily the most influential cookbook in the Colonies, as in England, during the latter half of the century. Among other cookbooks mentioned by her (in addition to some which saw American publication) are *The House-keeper's Pocket-book* by Sarah Harrison (1733); *The Experienced English House-keeper* by Elizabeth Raffald (1769; first American edition, virtually unchanged, 1801); and *The British Housewife* by Martha Bradley (*c.* 1770); *The Accomplisht Cook* by Robert May (1660); *The Country Housewife and Lady's Director* by Richard Bradley (1727); and *Acetaria: A Discourse on Sallets* by John Evelyn (1699).

It was not until 1742, it seems, that the first cookbook was published in the Colonies: *The Compleat Housewife* by E. Smith, printed by William Parks in Williamsburg. The recipes, "collected" from the fifth London edition, show

[5]Jane Carson, *Colonial Virginia Cookery.* Colonial Williamsburg, 1968.

no substantive changes from the 1727 edition and the work was already rather old-fashioned by the time it saw its only American publication, but it is invaluable for study of the first half of the century.

In 1772, *The Frugal Housewife* by Susannah Carter was published in Boston (London, 1772 [?]). The work saw six American editions. The handsome plates are by Paul Revere but there are no concessions to American practice until 1803.

The New Art of Cookery by Richard Briggs was published in Philadelphia in 1792 (London, 1788). It went through three editions.

In other words, until the close of the eighteenth century, extant cookbooks were imports or simple reprints of English works. The only peculiarly New World produce called for in them were those that had long been adopted in England: turkey, "French" beans, and sweet potatoes, well before 1600; white potatoes, by 1700; and Jerusalem artichokes, pineapple, chocolate, tomatoes, cayenne pepper, and vanilla, spottily and in varying degree, by mid-eighteenth century or so. As always, the printed word lagged behind usage; literature and manuscript recipes indicate earlier use in many instances.

American Cookery by Amelia Simmons, "An American Orphan," was published in Hartford in 1796. It is the first cookbook known to have been written by an American and to present recipes in English calling for *Indian meal* (corn meal),[6] which simply replaced fine oat grits or other grain in such English recipes as hearth cakes and boiled and baked puddings. Recipes for *Crookneck, or Winter Squash* and *Pompkin* puddings baked in crust also appear (see *pumpkins and squash*); pumpkins had long been made into pie in England but her custardy type became the all-American pie. Her recipe for *Soft Gingerbread to be baked in pans* is the earliest one I know for American style gingerbread as differentiated from the European type, more like our ginger snaps. She calls for *cramberry-sauce* to accompany roast turkey, continuing the virtually medieval English custom of serving preserved barberries with meat (both being red, hard, acid berries), as well

[6]But A. A. Parmentier in *Le Parfait Boulanger* (1778) had already given a recipe for a leavened bread of *maïs,* or *blé de Turquie* (Turkey wheat, a common name for Indian corn in Europe), made by the procedure "which is used in the Bearn," according to him. Just so, cornmeal was already replacing the meal of millet or chestnuts in *millas* and *polenta* in various parts of France and Italy, illustrating once again the historical tendency of people to use their own traditional recipes when confronted with unfamiliar produce.

as tarts of *cramberries*. She also employs some
interesting Americanisms: *Slapjack,* which I
take to be a colonial misreading of *flapjack* (*f*
and long *s* being confusingly similar), a regional
term for pancake in England (Norfolk, says Halliwell) that was recorded by 1600, according to
OED: slaw, from Dutch *sla,* salad (later pre-
ceded by *cole,* an old English word for cabbage,
parallel to Dutch *kool*); *cookey,* from Dutch
koekje, rather than the *little cake* of England;
and *Johny Cake, or Hoe Cake.* Her second edition (also 1796) includes patriotic recipes for *Independence Cake* and *Election Cake,* which
hardly differ from English seventeenth-century
"great cakes," and one for *Federal Pan Cakes*
calling for the typically American mixture of
Indian and rye meals. She also gives a recipe for
Chouder, but none for baked beans, a curious
omission.

But it is her recording of the use of *pearl ash*
(which see) as an expedient leavening that
strikes the most distinctively American note.
Mrs. Wilson in her well-documented introduction says that this is the first published example
of a practice pioneered by American women.
Would that they had not, because in the course of
the nineteenth century the use of chemicals in
American baking was to all but drive out traditional forms of aerating cakes and quick breads
such as yeast, natural fermentation, eggs, and

beating in air. Baked goods became ever puffier, softer, sweeter, and increasingly infected with the caustic aftertaste of chemical "baking powders," as they came to be called. It was a taste that Americans learned to love. Mrs. Randolph had scant use for it; see *Plebeian Gingerbread* (facsimile).

But the body of the Simmons work remains essentially English. (Indeed, her entire section on creams and syllabubs is lifted word for word from Susannah Carter's *The Frugal Housewife*.) For that matter, *American Cookery* is in many ways downright provincial when compared to works of popular English writers, who had been including occasional recipes for ice cream, pineapple, and tomatoes since mid-century and earlier, none of which Miss Simmons includes.

If Miss Simmons lacked originality—and she did—it may have been a virtue in this instance because the importance of *American Cookery* lies in its documentary value. Her corn meal recipes must be essentially those used by New Englanders since they first learned about maize from the Indians, for example. And in assessing her recipes, it must be remembered that all produce—vegetable and animal—raised on lean stony hill land has an intensity of flavor unmatched by that from "fat" bottom land and that all sea food from the cold New England waters has more flavor than that taken farther south.

The following quarter century was a dismal one in American cookbook history. *American Cookery* went through thirteen editions, a number of which did not bear her name and were very likely pirated. And there were two outrageous examples of plagiarism where the entire work, errata and all, was simply given a new title and author in each case.

In 1803, however, apparently responding to the challenge of the Simmons work, a new American edition of *The Frugal Housewife* by Susannah Carter appeared that contained an appendix of twenty-nine recipes, "adapted to the American mode of cookery," among them: *Whafles; Crullers,* from Dutch *krullen,* curls or twists; *Dough nuts,* nut-shaped as differentiated from crullers;[7] *To pickle Peppers;* and *Maple Sugar, Maple Molasses,* and *Maple Beer.* The recipes do not come from the Simmons work, even parallel ones. But two years later, the identical section appeared in the first American edition of *The Art of Cookery* by Hannah Glasse (Alexandria, 1805), including the same truncated directions for *"rearing Turkeys to advan-*

---

[7]This is the earliest appearance of either word that I have been able to trace but cakes and names must have been in long use because Washington Irving was to nostalgically recall them only a few years later in *The Legend of Sleepy Hollow,* often cited as first appearances (see *dough nuts*).

tage, translated from a Swedish book, entitled Rural Oeconomy," suggesting that in both instances, type had been set directly from an unknown common source, perhaps an almanac.

We must not overlook the considerable influence wielded by American editions of *A New System of Domestic Cookery* by "A Lady," Maria Eliza Rundell (Boston, 1807), which ran to at least thirty-seven editions (not including wholesale plagiarism), effectively replacing all eighteenth-century cookbooks as being rather old-fashioned, almost more in language than in content although there were indeed a number of first American appearances, I believe, of such innovations as *Bechamel, or white sauce* (veal, ham, aromatics, *roux,* "good broth," and cream), *Coffee Cream, much admired,* and *Chocolate Cream* (neither substance having previously been widely used except in beverages), as well as an expanded section of ice creams. From the New York edition on, her work included a number of American recipes, several of which were shamelessly lifted from the Simmons work, as *Johnny, or Hoe Cake, as made in Connecticut.* But there are also *Savannah Rice Cakes, Carolina Rice and Wheat Bread, Tomata Sauce* (effectively a catsup), and *Pepper Pot* (which turns out to be West Indian in origin; see *pepper pot*). There are also references to strictly American fish, such as *Sheeps Head, Rock Fish* or *Streaked Bass, Black Fish* (tautog), etc.

But nothing in the history of early American cookbooks quite prepares us for the sumptuous cuisine presented by Mary Randolph in *The Virginia House-wife* (1824). She brought her personal flair to everything she did but her reputation as the best cook in Virginia and the early success of her work indicate that her cookery was solidly based on Virginia produce and Virginia practice. Perhaps the most remarkable aspect of her cookery is its eclecticism, which flowed from the fascinating interplay of strikingly different influences that manifested themselves from the very beginning. A certain eclecticism has continued to mark American cookery, but never again with such eclat.

Underlying it all was the bounty of the lush Virginia tidelands. William Byrd, founder of Richmond and fellow of the Royal Society at a time when it was headed by Sir Isaac Newton, reports in *The Natural History of Virginia, or the Newly Discovered Eden* (1737) that Virginians had long been growing all manner of European fruits and vegetables as well as indigenous ones: ". . . very large and long asparagus of splendid flavor . . . beautiful cauliflower, chives, artichokes . . . many species of potatoes . . . smooth, curled and red lettuce . . . white and red garlic . . . two kinds of fennel," as well as several cabbages, pages of varieties of peas, beans, and all sorts of herbs and greens, some of which are difficult to find today—to wit, sorrel. He lists "many species of melons, such as watermelons and fragrant melons, Guinea [see *eggplant*], golden, orange, green, and several other sorts . . . several varieties of cucumbers, which are very sweet and good-tasting; four species of pumpkins; cashaws . . . simnals, horns, squashes are also very good. . . ." He lists scores of fruit and nut trees (twenty-four kinds of apple, explaining that he "wanted only to describe the best species of them"), including the native persimmon and pawpaw trees. This in addition to all sorts of berries; the indigenous Virginia strawberry, the *Little Scarlet* of today, had already been introduced into Europe, where previously only so-called wild ones (as *fraises des bois*) had been cultivated. As for meats, Byrd claims that the beef, veal, mutton, and pork were "always as good as the best European can be, since the pastures in this country are very fine." He speaks of "a large fat turkey-hen which weighs from thirty to forty and even more pounds" as selling for up to thirty pence. And he notes that "ordinary bread" was made of wheat but that old settlers often preferred Indian meal mixed with rice.

Robert Beverley, a historian and contemporary of Byrd, in his *History and Present State of Virginia* (1705), also remarks that "in Gentlemen's Houses . . . some rather chose the Pone [over wheat bread], which is the bread made of

Indian meal," adding that the word came from Indian *Oppone*. (Captain John Smith noted this ash cake by name in *A Map of Virginia,* 1612.) Beverley devotes a chapter to Indian agriculture and food that is of rare importance. After listing scores of fish, he reports that before the English came, fish were so plentiful that Indian children would take them with pointed sticks, a telling commentary. He records the little known story of French efforts to make wine as early as 1622, which "far excell'd their own country of *Languedoc.*" Later, the Huguenots tried yet again, producing a "Noble strong-bodied Claret, of a curious flavour." The French finally forsook their wines; as Beverley points out, wine grapes prefer gravelly slopes and do not do well alongside the pine tree. He also reports that, "Hogs [brought over by early colonists] swarm like Vermine upon the Earth, and are often accounted as such," not always being included in estate inventories. "The Hogs run where they list, and find their own Support in the Woods, without any Care of the Owner." Those pigs, nourished on acorns, fallen fruits, and roots, must have made wonderful eating. Small wonder that the quality of Virginia ham early became celebrated. I have not mentioned the long lists of game, feathered and furred, given by the writers, nor grains, nor dairy products.

Virginia was indeed a newfound Eden. And if

Beverley's prescient admonitions on the dangers of large plantations of a single crop fell on deaf ears, that reckoning was to come later. Certainly the myriad array of produce available to Virginians in the day of Mary Randolph had only been further enriched by "new" products—most conspicuously tomatoes—as evidenced by the meticulous records kept by Jefferson in his gardening manual and even more pertinently by his notations on arrivals in the Washington market during his terms of presidency, 1801–1809 (see *Appendix V*). And, industrialization had not yet exacted its toll in food quality; pollution was minimal and milling was still blessedly archaic (see *flour* and *corn meal*). Also, from the very beginning, wealthy Virginians imported vast quantities of oranges, almonds, wine, sugar and its byproducts, coffee, tea, etc.

Let us move from the larder to the kitchen. In the richly worked tapestry of Virginia, the warp was English, as surely if not so plainly as in that of New England. And there are English recipe titles by the score in *The Virginia House-wife*, any number of which are virtually identical to their parallel recipes from Elizabethan and Jacobean times as they are found in *Martha Washington's Booke of Cookery,* for example:

Macaroone, Slip, Jumbals, Curd Pudding, Curds and Cream, Barley Cream, Sippet Pudding, Shrewsbury Cakes, To Pickle Oysters, Tansey Pudding, To Collar a Flank of Beef, and *Almond Pudding,* to name but a few of Mrs. Randolph's recipes. Her recipe for *Green Pea Soup* calls for mint, exactly as does *Pease Porrage of Greene Pease* in the ancient manuscript, and her way of garnishing braised *Fricando of Beef* with sorrel or spinach and fried meat balls is quintessentially seventeenth-century English cookery. Her basic bread method is English, as is her puff paste procedure, as distinct from French practice (as discussed in *Martha Washington's Booke of Cookery*). Even her prodigious hand with wine is a direct legacy from English cookery, where its lavish use had been taken for granted since medieval times, a gift of the Normans. (There was considerable production of wine in both England and Normandy in earlier times, not of very high quality perhaps, but much used in cookery.) And some of the exotic-sounding preparations seem to have first become known through English cookbooks (see *Oil Mangos,* in glossary, for example).

But there are surprises. The two heads of garlic in her wonderfully redolent *Beef-a-la Mode* (see facsimile) might be explained by having gotten the recipe from French sources rather than English cookbooks, where it had been appearing innocent of garlic all through the eighteenth century. But what of "a few cloves of garlic" in her recipe for *Scotch Collops of Veal* (*scotched* or scored, not Scottish), a standby in the English kitchen already for centuries? All evidence indicates that while during the seventeenth and eighteenth centuries the structure of parallel preparations closely followed that set down in English cookbooks, Virginians had become accustomed to headier seasonings than were the English, or New Englanders, for that matter. And it is not merely a question of garlic, which Mrs. Randolph uses with consummate skill, or even of borrowings, but of an elemental change in palate.

In attempting to identify the various strands in Virginia cookery, let us examine as best we can the local Indian contributions, the most important of which was maize, or Indian corn. It had an incalculable effect on Virginia food habits, threatening the dominance of wheat, even among the wealthy. Then there were sweet potatoes, squash (see *pumpkins and squash*) beans, and various fruits and nuts, some of which I have mentioned above, as well as medicinal barks and herbs. Needless to say, the settlers learned from the Indians how to grow these products and prepare them for keeping.

That said, I find less *direct* Indian influence in Virginia cookery—at least in Mrs. Randolph's rather aristocratic kitchen—than one might expect. That is, many American products had either been known in England well before the days of colonization or resembled already familiar products sufficiently so that old methods continued (but see *pearl ash*). This was true even with maize to some extent. Beverley, for example, reports that Indian pone was wrapped in leaves, covered with ashes, then heaped with coals and so baked. Cottage cookery was ill-recorded in England, as elsewhere, but various ash and hearth cakes are well nigh universal; in Britain, the humble resorted to them as a way of shunning the manor oven, and some have survived in this day, often made of coarsely milled oats, baked on irons propped up in front of the fire, much as described in early *Johnny Cake* recipes.

According to Beverley, it was "very common with [the Indians] to boil Fish as well as Flesh with their *Homony;* this is *Indian* corn soaked, broken in a Mortar, husked, and then boil'd in Water over a gentle Fire, for ten or twelve hours, to the consistence of Furmity" (long-cooked cracked wheat porridge). This method differs in no significant way from ancient pottages that survived well into recorded history in England, as elsewhere, and was by that time accomplished in European pots. (William Wood in *New Englands Prospect,* 1634, reports that the local Indians had "large Kettles which they traded for with the *French* long since, and doe still buy of the *English.* . . .") Roasting and broiling were done "by laying the Meat itself upon the Coals, [or] by laying it upon Sticks rais'd upon Forks at some distance above the live Coals, which heats more gently, and drys up the *Gravy;* this they, and we also from them, call Barbecueing."[8] But until mid-nineteenth century, when the iron range revolutionized cookery, the English in Virginia continued to roast their meat in front of the fire as they had in England, so that the precious juices might collect in a dripping pan safely away from the fierce heat instead of being lost in the fire.

Outdoor festive events were quite another matter, and the barbecue became a popular institution in the South. The dryness of the meat noted by Beverley came to be compensated for by basting it with various mixtures. I cannot date this, but by the time of Mrs. Randolph's recipe *To Barbecue Shote* (facsimile), we find the meat baked in a sauce; in a sense, the sauce had already become the characterizing element of a barbecue, as it still is pretty much today. Her

[8]The word comes from Haitian Taino *barbacoa* by way of Spanish and originally referred to the wooden framework *(Webster).* It seems to have been in early use among southern Atlantic Indians.

rich sauce of *Mushroom Catsup* (see facsimile) and wine is eighteenth-century English, and this continues as late as Mrs. Tyree's version in 1879. Today's fiery vinegary barbecue sauces may have originated in Creole customs.

No, as important as local Indian contributions were, the transformation of Virginia cookery cannot primarily be attributed to them, or we would have expected parallel changes to have taken place in New England as well, where there was also considerable Indian influence. It is only when we ask whose hands did the cooking that we get a satisfactory answer. New England women were dissidents who for the most part did their own work; any servants tended also to be English. But among the gentry of Virginia, black women slaves traditionally did the cooking. They had brought with them from Africa long familiarity with a number of hitherto little known products whose very use came to characterize southern cookery: *gumbo, eggplant, field peas,* benne (an African name for sesame), yams (which resemble New World sweet potatoes in culinary use, although not at all related),[9] and possibly *tomatoes.* Among other products, sorghum and watermelon came

[9]In a letter to Anthony Giannini in 1786 from Paris, Jefferson orders seed for: "the sweet potatoe. I mean that kind which the negroes tend so generally."

from Africa and bananas were known there.

In addition, many of these black cooks had passed through the way station of the West Indies—or knew those who had—where they picked up a number of dishes (see *gumbo, pepper pot,* and *a-la-daube,* for example) and tricks of seasoning from the exuberant Creole cuisines of the islanders. The Caribs had early been all but exterminated but any remaining women would have mingled with the black slaves who were brought in, and so certain traces remained, particularly in products used (various *Capsicum* peppers, most notably, and very likely tomatoes). More important, the vast majority of the populations were black, and they had made their own colorful, irreverent adaptations of the cuisines of their respective masters, be they French, English, or Spanish, or other, with inevitable mingling.

These creole cuisines were to color Virginia cookery to an extent which has not been fully appreciated, I think, because in addition to actual borrowings, there is the thumb print that each cook leaves on a recipe, even within the same culture, no matter how skilled she may be or how faithfully she follows the recipe. The Chinese call this phenomenon *wok presence.* It's a question of the temperature of cooking fats, of generosity in measuring, of "nose," not to mention palate, of timing, of patience, of scores of nearly indefinable qualities that go into creating a dish, all of which are formed by years of working with food. And so it was that even when thoroughly English dishes were cooked by hands that had known other products, other cuisines, the result would never be quite English in the way that the same dishes would be in New England, for instance, ignoring for the moment differences in produce. The black presence was infinitely more subtle in Virginia cookery than in that of New Orleans or the West Indies, but no less real for that, and the culture was sufficiently imbued with it to condition the palate of the entire community. And that warmth of traditional Virginia cookery constitutes its charm.

Mrs. Randolph left her own imprint on these Virginia recipes, to be sure; her perceptiveness and culinary curiosity added new dimensions to Virginia cookery. But she was working within an already sophisticated cuisine, a harmonious interweaving of colorful Indian, African black, and Creole strands on the warp of the fine cookery of seventeenth- and eighteenth-century England, all of which had been transformed in various ways in response to local produce and talents. In short, an authentic American cuisine.

Among other borrowings, there are perhaps fewer recipes from French cuisine than one might expect; most French titles refer to English or Creole adaptations of long standing, *blanc manger, French rolls, a-la-daube,* etc. But there are *Fondus, Bell Fritters, Matelote* and an early recipe in English for genuine French fries, *To Fry Sliced Potatoes* among others. Possible sources are legion.

There is a group of Spanish recipes of exceptional interest: *Gaspacho—Spanish; Spanish Method of Dressing Giblets,* a version of the ancient *pepitoria,* originally a fricassee of giblets *(Appendix II); Eggs and Tomatoes,* effectively a *piperade; Olla—A Spanish Dish;* and *Ropa Veija—Spanish,* properly *Ropa Vieja,* old clothes, a way of using cold meat that was to enter Virginia cookery, surviving in cookbooks and manuscripts through the nineteenth century. The recipes are perfectly traditional and must have been personally collected because such homey recipes were not deemed worthy of entry in Spanish cookbooks, which were exceedingly sparse in any event. I suggest that they may well have come from Harriet Randolph Hackley, Mary Randolph's sister, who seems to have spent some time in Cadiz. On April 10, 1809, Jefferson noted in his *Garden Book* that he had planted "apricot stones . . . they came from mrs Hackley Cadiz" (whose brother had married Martha Jefferson). Again on March 17, 1810, he planted "hardshelled sweet Almonds from Cadiz," very likely from the same source.

Mrs. Randolph's *Dish of Curry after the East Indian Manner* may indeed be from Indian rather than English sources; she gives a recipe for *Curry Powder.* Her Italian recipe for *Polenta* is interesting; less so are *Vermecelli* and *Macaroni,* the latter a prototype of the limp factory macaroni and processed cheese that was to spread like a plague over the country.

Conventional wisdom has it that early Americans paid scant attention to vegetables and that they cooked them to death. Mrs. Randolph gives instructions for using forty some vegetables and seventeen aromatic herbs. And a glance at Jefferson's notes on produce for sale at the Washington market, even in winter, should settle the question of availability of vegetables for those who did not themslves garden (see *Appendix V*).

In Mrs. Randolph's directions for asparagus, she cautions: "Great care must be taken to watch the exact time of their becoming tender; take them just at that instant, and they will have their true flavour and colour; *a minute or two more boiling destroys both.*" [*Emphasis added.*] As for spinach, "a few minutes will boil it sufficiently." And Hannah Glasse had been preaching the same gospel for decades: "All things that are green should have a little crispness, for if they are over-boiled, they neither have any sweetness or beauty."

It was not until canning became a popular method of preservation around mid-nineteenth century that we find those horrid recipes for overboiled vegetables. Nobody raised on canned spinach or string beans can possibly know what good food is.

(I have not discussed Mrs. Randolph's methods of conservation, partly because of space and also because her recipes are pretty much as they had been for centuries in English cookbooks. But I must note that the traditional corning, smoking, drying, pickling, and preserving with sugar methods used by her and her forebears, produced food of far greater interest than the mushy canned and frozen foods of today. This is because the ancient methods actually intensify flavor and enhance textural interest. Hams, sausages, salt and dried fish, pickled meats and vegetables, dried legumes of all kinds, and preserved fruits, are all the result of these "primitive" methods. We have retained a taste for them in spite of "progress." Mind you, their quality is rapidly eroding, but if we search it out, we can still find genuine country ham, especially in Virginia and the Carolinas.)

"No meat can be well roasted," Mrs. Randolph writes, "except on a spit turned by a jack, and before a steady clear fire—*other methods are no better than baking*." [*Emphasis added*.] Roasting entails the formation of a lightly caramelized crust at the outset; the heat must be sufficient to "seize" the meat, then reduced in order to finish cooking it without burning, all in proportion to the size and nature of the cut involved. The whole point of a roast is to achieve the contrast of the outside crust and its intense flavor with the beautifully rare juicy interior. Perfect roasting requires great care and perceptiveness; "roasted to a turn" is not just a pretty phrase.

Mrs. Randolph gives no roasting time for butcher meats except to note that "Beef and mutton must not be roasted as much as veal, lamb, or pork," but Miss Simmons, back in 1796, said very firmly of roast beef that "rare done is the healthiest and the taste of this age." This early American taste for rare meats is borne out by Mrs. Randolph's directions on poultry: *Large Fowls* will be near an hour in roasting," *Young Chickens* "will take a quarter of an hour," and *Wild Ducks or Teal* will roast in twenty minutes, "if the fire be good." As for turkey, "if it be of a middle size [perhaps twelve pounds], it will require an hour and a quarter to roast." *Amen*.

The first terrible blow to the art of roasting in America was the general acceptance of the iron kitchen range in mid-nineteenth century. Even so, it is difficult to understand how a people who had inherited the English tradition of roasting could have been conditioned in just a few decades to accept the grey sodden stringy "roasts" foisted upon us by Fannie Farmer (1896) and the long line of home economists who followed.

(Meat does not properly roast in an oven because of steaminess. Some meats tolerate such steaminess, indeed require it, but they are "baked meats," *not* roasts. By using high oven temperatures, it is possible to nearly approximate spit roasting, but it requires great care and watchfulness. I oven-roast a fifteen-pound turkey to succulent perfection in one and a half hours; all of Mrs. Randolph's roasting times may be taken as valid guides.)

While we are on meats, I would like to draw attention to Mrs. Randolph's recipe *To Toast a Ham*. I cannot date the unfortunate sweet glazing of Virginia ham that has become so prevalent, but as late as 1879, none of Mrs. Tyree's contributed recipes give such a version. I would like to see a return to traditional methods. Mrs. Randolph is, however, unhelpful in the preparation of the ham: it must be well scrubbed, soaked for twelve hours in cool water, then kept at an *imperceptible* simmer until *just* tender (the least bubbling risks making the meat stringy), then cooled in its liquor before continuing.

Her recipes *To Boil a Turkey* and *To Boil Fowls*

are rather unusual in method and illustrate once again the short cooking times that she favored.

I have not yet discussed the important subject of Mrs. Randolph's use of liaisons. For the most part, she relies on the richness of her sauces to provide the requisite body. Often she enhances this effect by stirring in additional butter before serving, a technique now identified only with French cuisine but one that characterized the golden age of English cookery, the seventeenth century, as well. (This whipping in of butter was the favored technique in *Martha Washington's Booke of Cookery,* for instance.) But Mrs. Randolph was a child of her time so her use of butter is often "fortified" in its thickening power by the addition of flour in a *beurre manié,* a technique popular with Mrs. Glasse, who thickened her *Oyster-Sauce* with "a Pound of Butter rolled in a little Flour" (1755). Mrs. Randolph does not often give proportions, but in her *Fricassee of Small Chickens (Appendix IV)* she calls for eight tablespoons of butter kneaded with two tablespoons of flour, and in her recipe *To Melt Butter,* she calls for two teaspoons (actually one-half tablespoon) for the same amount of butter. Classic proportions call for equal amounts of butter and flour by volume. When appropriate, she calls for using *brown flour* in this technique.

Mrs. Randolph avoids the classic *roux* although it had been becoming increasingly popular in English cookbooks during the eighteenth century; Mrs. Glasse uses it in her recipes for *Cullis* in 1755, for example, but Mrs. Randolph's parallel recipe for *Gravy* is unthickened. Most often, she uses *gravy* in the old sense of running juices of roast meat, but the meaning was changing; in any event, it was unthickened unless so specified.

Occasionally, Mrs. Randolph resorts to using egg yolk as an enriching liaison or throwing in a few bread crumbs for a little body, both old English techniques. The entire section on *Sauces* (beginning page 108 in facsimile) is worthy of study, to which should be added: *Sauce for a Goose, Onion Sauce,* oyster *Sauce for a Turkey,* bread *Sauce for a Turkey, White Sauce for Fowls, Egg Sauce, To Dress Ducks with Juice or Oranges* (under *poultry,* beginning page 79 in facsimile), and *Sauce a-la-Creme* (page 105 in facsimile), as well as those recipes where the sauce is an integral part of the dish. (For wine in cookery, see index.)

Among Mrs. Randolph's desserts, the ice cream recipes deserve special mention (beginning page 174 of facsimile). She gives twenty-two flavors, an inordinate number for the period, not including variations involving the substitution of custard for heavy cream in certain recipes: "If rich cream can be procured, it will be infinitely better," she notes. Most of the recipes are of exceptional quality and a number of them I believe to be altogether original with her. They are best frozen in cranked freezers. For the rest, the recipes are for unexceptional English sweets of high quality, with one curious oversight: there is no recipe for cheese-cake, which had been popular in England since early fifteenth century, at least, and remained so in the Colonies.

All of this cookery was carried out in kitchens that had changed but little in centuries. In Virginia, the kitchen was typically a separate building, for reasons of safety, summer heat, and the smells and brouhaha of the kitchen. The heart of the kitchen was the great fireplace, where roasting was conducted and where cauldrons of water and broth were usually simmering away. Swinging cranes and various ingenious devices made for rather more flexibility in temperature control than the modern housewife might imagine, but the labor was backbreaking. The *Dutch oven* and the *chafing dish* provided some measure of relief in this regard, as well as means of achieving certain niceties of detail in the cookery. The brick oven was usually alongside the fireplace. Home refrigeration had undergone some modernization (see *Appendix III*). Readers who are interested in the practical organization of early Virginia kitchens are referred to Jane Carson's excellent work.

Mrs. Randolph was a fine practitioner who knew her way about the kitchen but the actual cooking and toil fell to black women. (Mrs. Randolph indicates as much in her *Introduction;* other sources confirm this.) When slavery was ended at long last, and more and more housewives everywhere had to do more and more of their own work, it is easy to see why the great fireplace gave way to the kitchen range. Neither bread nor traditional pastries baked half so well in the new iron oven (the refraction patterns and "dry" heat of the brick oven make for ideal baking conditions). And the baleful effect of the change on "roasting" methods was even more dramatic. But the iron range was thought to be more convenient, and progress had its way.

At about the same time, new milling methods were impoverishing the flour, chemical baking powders were infecting baked goods, and canning was beginning to displace traditional methods of conservation. These changes came little by little and were sold as labor-saving measures. As with today's "convenience" foods, the labor saved was largely illusory and the costs were dear, not only in actual price but in decline of quality. But here again, progress had its way.

The finest cookbook writers of the second quarter of that century, Eliza Leslie (*Directions for Cookery*, 1837) and Sarah Rutledge (*The Carolina Housewife*, 1847) chief among them, were strongly influenced by *The Virginia House-wife* and kept the faith. (Actual plagiarism increased as its true influence declined.) Their works were still the collections of the "secrets" of perceptive cooks for the edification of other housewives.

Ironically, if inevitably, the quality of cooking declined as the quality of produce declined and had more need of skilled cooks. The works of the latter half of the century are fascinating because they document this decline and the increasing tendency of writers to give way to expediency, until by the end of the century most had become handmaidens of industry, wittingly or no.

During this period, the use of wine in cookery declined, as did the use of all manner of aromatics, but the use of flour in sauces and of sugar in cakes and breads increased rapidly. Cooking times for both meats and vegetables were getting longer and longer; certain vegetables (sorrel and broccoli, for instance) and most herbs, as well as shallots and even garlic, all but vanished from the kitchen. As if to compensate, the use of harsh seasonings such as red peppers (previously used by fine cooks in such a way as to heighten flavor) or commercial condiments such as worcestershire sauce were increasingly called upon in cookbooks in steadily increasing amounts. Even the use of olive oil fell back under the onslaught of various tasteless "vegetable" oils just as the use of lard and butter retreated before various horrid substitutes. So much so, that when Americans were gradually reintroduced to the wonders of using wine, herbs, garlic and shallots, and olive oil in cookery around mid-twentieth century, it seemed wildly exotic. Broccoli had made a comeback with the influx of Italian immigrants in the 1920s; it is only recently that shallots have become fairly common; it is still difficult to find sorrel. But all these products were commonplace in the first decades of our republic.

Nor was this slide confined to the more industrialized north. A look at *The New Southern Cookery-Book* (1871) by Mrs. Porter, of "Prince George Court-House, Virginia," shows that a number of vegetables and herbs used by Mrs. Randolph seem already to have fallen from use; I find mention of neither garlic nor shallot; and spinach is to "simmer slowly for about an hour." But she gives nearly 200 recipes for sweet cakes and nearly 100 for breads, most of which are aerated with soda or pearl ash. This is in addition to more than 200 recipes for dessert pastries and puddings. The contributed recipes in Mrs. Tyree's *Housekeeping in Old Virginia* (1879) confirm the trend, if with a touch of nostalgia. (The Creole cuisine of New Orleans withstood this decline for decades longer than did that of the country as a whole. I feel that it was the highly aromatic cuisine of that city that made it seem so "foreign," even a bit sinful, to so many Americans. Southern black cookery is less documented, but it also seems to have suffered less.)

By the end of the century with Fannie Farmer, there were no more questions because she, and those who followed, had lost touch with the fragrances, tastes, and textures of the past. Succeeding editions of her *Boston Cooking-School Cook Book* (1896) saw ever-increasing amounts of sugar in bread and salad dressings, and in the inevitable substitution of sugary lemon gelatine full of artificial flavoring and coloring for traditional aspic mixtures; Jell-O was introduced in 1897 and swept the country, irremediably warping the American palate. We had entered the twentieth century and Fannie Farmer, a remarkably imperceptive cook possessed of a raging sweet tooth, was to become the patron saint of the American kitchen. A pity that it was not Mary Randolph.

Perhaps it is not too late. There is much talk of

returning to our "roots." We are, to be sure, a multi-national people, but we were in the days of Mary Randolph as well. It is not so much a question of faithfully following her recipes as of emulating her spirit in the kitchen, her understanding of the relationship between the nature and quality of produce and cookery, and her skillful working of the many strands present in early Virginia cookery. This is what makes her cookery so thoroughly American; it constitutes a lesson that we would do well to study.

A note for modern cooks. "Profusion is not elegance," Mrs. Randolph advises, and this may be taken to apply to needless complications of a dish as well as to the composition of a menu. With few exceptions (the turtle recipes most notably), her recipes are of admirable simplicity of concept, clearly expressed, and full of perceptive observations. Now that the most toilsome aspects of kitchen work have largely been banished, the only problems that busy cooks will encounter is that of finding produce of suitable quality. (See *weights & measures* for questions of that nature.) I can only suggest searching out small-scale traditional operations for hams, flour, cornmeal, and so on; they do exist here and there. But what can I tell people who have never tasted *real* cream? Commercial cream has now "progressed" beyond the point of no-return. I count myself fortunate because I can still find "heavy cream" that is not embalmed to last for months, but no self-respecting Jersey cow would recognize it. Perhaps if those of us who know the difference raised a ruckus, we might convince the dairy interests to offer the real thing. In the meanwhile, try to find the rare aficionado who keeps a small herd of Jersey cows. (Additional suggestions are given under certain individual products in the glossary.)

Now let us turn to *The Virginia House-wife* (1824) by Mary Randolph.

The Facsimile

THE

VIRGINIA HOUSE-WIFE.

———

METHOD IS THE SOUL OF MANAGEMENT.

———

WASHINGTON :

:::::.:::::::::::

PRINTED BY DAVIS AND FORCE, (FRANKLIN'S HEAD,)

PENNSYLVANIA AVENUE.

1824.

DISTRICT OF COLUMBIA, to wit:

Be it remembered, That on the seventh day of May, in the year of our Lord one thousand eight hundred and twenty-four, and of the independence of the United States of America the forty-eighth, Henry Stone, of the said District, has deposited in the office of the Clerk of the District Court for the District of Columbia, the title of a Book, the right whereof he claims as Proprietor, in the words following, to wit:

"*The Virginia House Wife. Method is the soul of management.*"

In conformity to the act of the Congress of the United States, entitled "An act for the encouragement of learning, by securing the copies of *Maps, Charts,* and *Books,* to the authors and proprietors of such copies during the times therein mentioned;" and also to the act, entitled "An act supplementary to an act, entitled ' An act for the encouragement of learning, by securing the copies of *Maps, Charts,* and *Books,* to the authors and proprietors of such copies during the times therein mentioned,' and extending the benefits thereof to the arts of designing, engraving, and etching historical and other *prints.*"

In testimony whereof, I have hereunto set my hand, (L. S.) and affixed the public seal of my office, the day and year aforesaid.

EDM : I. LEE,
Clerk of the District Court for the District of Columbia

CONTENTS.

CONTENTS.

A 2

CONTENTS.

viii CONTENTS.

DISHES FOR LENT,
And other fast days.

PREFACE.

The difficulties I encountered when I first entered on the duties of a House-keeping. life, from the want of books sufficiently clear and concise, to impart knowledge to a Tyro, compelled me to study the subject, and by actual experiment, to reduce every thing, in the culinary line, to proper weights and measures. This method I found not only to diminish the necessary attention and labour, but to be also economical; for, when the ingredients employed, were given in just proportions, the article made, was always equally good. The government of a family, bears a Liliputian resemblance to the government of a nation. The contents of the Treasury must be known, and great care taken to keep the expenditures from being equal to the receipts. A regular system must be introduced

*into each department, which may be modified
until matured, and should then pass into an
inviolable law.   The grand arcanum of management lies in three simple rules:—" Let
every thing be done at the proper time, keep
every thing in its proper place, and put every
thing to its proper use."   If the mistress of
a family will every morning examine minute-
ly, the different departments of her house-
hold, she must detect errors in their infant
state, when they can be corrected with ease.
But a few days' growth gives them gigantic
strength, and Disorder, with all her attendant
evils, are introduced.   Early rising is also
essential to the good government of a family.
A late breakfast deranges the whole business
of the day, and throws a portion of it on
the next, which opens the door for confusion
to enter.   The greater part of the following
receipts have been written from memory,
where they were impressed by long continued practice.   Should they prove service-*

able to the young inexperienced housekeeper, it will add greatly to that gratification which an extensive circulation of the
work will be likely to confer.

M. RANDOLPH.

WASHINGTON, *January*, 1824.

VIRGINIA HOUSE WIFE.

DIRECTIONS FOR CURING BEEF.

Prepare your brine in the middle of October, after the following manner: Get a thirty gallon cask, take out one head, drive in the bung and put some pitch on it, to prevent leaking. See that the cask is quite tight and clean. Put into it one pound of salt-petre, powdered, fifteen quarts of salt, and fifteen gallons of cold water; stir it frequently, until dissolved, throw over the cask a thick cloth, to keep out the dust: look at it often and take off the scum. These proportions have been accurately ascertained—fifteen gallons of cold water will exactly hold, in solution, fifteen quarts of good clean Liverpool salt, and one pound of salt-petre: this brine will be strong enough to bear up an egg: if more salt be added, it

B

will fall to the bottom without strengthening the brine, the water being already saturated. This brine will cure all the beef, which a private family can use in the course of the winter, and requires nothing more to be done to it except occasionally skimming the dross that rises. It must be kept in a cool, dry place. For salting your beef, get a molasses hogshead and saw it in two, that the beef may have space to lie on; bore some holes in the bottom of these tubs, and raise them on one side about an inch, that the bloody brine may run off.

Be sure that your beef is newly killed—rub each piece very well with good Liverpool salt—a vast deal depends upon rubbing the salt into every part—it is unnecessary to put salt-petre on it; sprinkle a good deal of salt on the bottom of the tub. When the beef is well salted, lay it in the tub, and be sure you put the fleshy side downward.— Put a great deal of salt on your beef after it is packed in the tub; this protects it from animals who might eat, if they could smell, it, and does not waste the salt, for the beef can only dissolve a certain portion. You must let the beef lie in salt ten days, then take it out, brush off the salt and wipe it with a damp cloth ; put it in the brine with a bit of board and weight to keep it under. In about ten days, it will look red and be fit for the table, but it will be red much sooner when the brine becomes older. The best time to begin to salt beef is the latter end of October, if the weather be cool, and from that time have it in succession. When your beef is taken out of the tub, stir the salt about to dry, that it may be ready for the next pieces. Tongues are cured in the same manner.

TO DRY BEEF FOR SUMMER USE.

The best pieces for this purpose are the thin briskets, or that part of the plate which is farthest from the shoulder of the animal, the round and rib pieces, that are commonly used for roasting. These should not be cut with long ribs, and the back-bones must be sawed off as close as possible, that the piece may lay flat in the dish. About the middle of February, select your beef from an animal, well fatted with corn, and which, when killed, will weigh one hundred and fifty per quarter—larger oxen are always coarse.—Salt the pieces as directed, let them lie one fortnight, then put them in brine, where they must remain three weeks; take them out at the end of the time, wipe them quite dry, rub them over with bran, and hang them in a cool, dry, and, if possible, dark place, that the flies may not get to them : they must be suspended, and not allowed to touch any thing. It will be necessary, in the course of the summer, to look them over occasionally, and after a long wet season, to lay them in the sun a few hours. Your tongues may be dried in the same manner: Make a little hole in the root, run a twine through it and suspend it. These dried meats must be put in a good quantity of water, to soak the night before they are to be used. In boiling, it is absolutely necessary to have a large quantity of water, to put the beef in while the water is cold, to boil steadily, skimming the pot, until the bones are ready to fall out ; and, if a tongue, till the skin peels off with perfect ease : the skin must also be taken from the beef. The housekeeper who will buy good ox beef, and follow these directions exactly, may be assured of always having delicious beef on her table. Ancient prejudice has established a notion, that meat killed in the decrease of the moon, will draw up when cooked. The true cause of this shrinking, may be found in the old age of the animal, or in its diseased state, at the time of killing. The best age is from three to five years.

Few persons are aware of the injury they sustain, by eating the flesh of diseased animals. None but the Jewish butchers, who are paid exclusively for it, attend to this important circumstance. The best rule for judging that I have been able to discover, is the colour of the fat. When the fat of beef is a high shade of yellow, I reject it. If the fat of veal, mutton, lamb, or pork, have the slightest tinge of yellow, I avoid it as diseased. The same rule holds good when applied to poultry.

—

TO CURE BACON.

Hogs are in the highest perfection, from two and a half to four years old, and make

B 2

the best bacon, when they do not weigh more
than one hundred and fifty or sixty at farthest: They should be fed with corn, six
weeks, at least, before they are killed, and the
shorter distance they are driven to market,
the better will their flesh be. To secure
them against the possibility of spoiling, salt
them before they get cold: take out the
chine or back-bone from the neck to the tail,
cut the hams, shoulders and middlings; take
the ribs from the shoulders, and the leaf
fat from the hams: have such tubs as are
directed for beef, rub a large table-spoonful
of salt petre on the inside of each ham, for
some minutes, then rub both sides well with
salt, sprinkle the bottom of the tub with salt,
lay the hams with the skin downward, and
put a good deal of salt between each layer;
salt the shoulders and middlings in the same
manner, but less salt-petre is necessary : cut
the jowl or chop from the head, and rub it
with salt and salt-petre.   You should cut off
the feet just above the knee-joint; take off
the ears and noses, and lay them in a large
tub of cold water for souse.   When the jowls
have been in salt two weeks, hang them up

to smoke—do so with the shoulders and middlings at the end of three weeks, and the
hams at the end of four. If they remain
longer in salt they will be hard. Remember
to hang the hams and shoulders with the
hocks down to preserve the juices. Make a
good smoke every morning, and be careful
not to have a blaze ; the smoke-house should
stand alone, for any additional heat will spoil
the meat. During the hot weather, beginning the first of April, it should be occasionally taken down, examined, rubbed with
hickory ashes, and hung up again.

The generally received opinion that salt-
petre hardens meat, is entirely erroneous :—
it tends greatly to prevent putrefaction, but
will not make it hard ; neither will laying in
brine five or six weeks in cold weather, have
that effect, but remaining in salt too long,
will certainly draw off the juices, and harden
it. Bacon should be boiled in a large quantity of wa'er, and a ham is not done sufficiently, till the bone on the under part comes
off with ease. New bacon requires much
longer boiling than that which is old.

TO MAKE SOUSE.

Let all the pieces you intend to souse, remain covered with cold water twelve hours; then wash them out, wipe off the blood, and put them again in fresh water; soak them in this manner, changing the water frequently, and keeping it in a cool place, till the blood is drawn away; scrape and clean each piece perfectly nice, mix some meal with water, add salt to it, and boil your souse gently, until you can run a straw into the skin with ease. Do not put too much in the pot for it will boil to pieces and spoil the appearance. The best way is, to boil the feet in one pot, the ears and noses in another, and the heads in a third; these should be boiled till you can take all the bones out; let them get cold, season the insides with pepper, salt, and a little nutmeg; make it in a tight roll, sew it up close in a cloth, and press it lightly. Mix some more meal and cold water, just enough to look white; add salt, and one fourth of vinegar; put your souse in different pots, and keep it well covered with this mixture, and closely stopped. It will be necessary to renew this liquor, every two or three weeks. Let your souse get quite cold after boiling, before you put it in the liquor, and be sure to use pale coloured vinegar, or the souse will be dark. Some cooks singe the hair from the feet, *etcetera*, but this destroys the colour :—good souse will always be white.

TO CURE HERRINGS.

The best method for preserving herrings, and which may be followed with ease, for a small family, is to take the brine left of your winter stock for beef, to the fishing place, and when the seine is hauled, to pick out the largest herrings, having roes, and throw them alive into the brine ; let them remain twenty-four hours, take them out and lay them on sloping planks, that the brine may drain off ; have a tight barrel, put some coarse allum salt in the bottom, then put in a layer of herrings—take care not to bruise them ; sprinkle over it allum salt and some salt-petre, then fish salt and salt-petre, till the barrel is full ; keep a board over it. Should they not make brine enough to cover them in a few weeks, you must add some, for they will be rusty if not kept under brine. The proper time to salt them is when they have been up the rivers long enough to fatten : the scales will adhere closely to a lean herring, but will be loose on a fat one—the former is not fit to be eaten. Do not be sparing of salt when you put them up. When they are to be used, take a few out of brine, soak them an hour or two, scale them nicely, pull off the gills, and the only entrail they have will come with them ; wash them clean and hang them up to dry. When to be broiled, take half a sheet of white paper, rub it over with butter, put the herring in, double the edges securely, and broil, without burning, it. The brine the herrings drink before they die, has a wonderful effect in preserving their juices :—When one or two years old, they are equal to anchovies.

TO CORN BEEF IN HOT WEATHER.

Take a piece of thin brisket or plate, cut out the ribs nicely, rub it on both sides well with two large spoonsful of pounded saltpetre ; pour on it a gill of molasses and a quart of salt; rub them both in; put it in a vessel just large enough to hold it, but not tight, for the bloody brine must run off as it makes, or the meat will spoil. Let it be well covered top, bottom, and sides, with the molasses and salt. In four days you may boil it, tied up in a cloth, with the salt, &c. about it: when done, take the skin off nicely, and serve it up. If you have an ice-house or refrigerator, it will be best to keep it there.— A fillet or breast of veal, and a leg or rack of mutton, are excellent done in the same way.

—

GENERAL OBSERVATIONS.

In roasting butcher's meat, be careful not to run the spit through the nice parts: let the piece lie in water one hour, then wash it out, wipe it perfectly dry, and put it on the spit. Set it before a clear, steady, fire; sprinkle some salt on it, and when it becomes hot, baste it for a time with salt and water; then put a good spoonful of nice lard into the dripping-pan, and when melted, continue to baste with it. When your meat, of whatever kind,

has been down some time, but before it begins to look brown, cover it with paper, and
baste on it; when it is nearly done, take off
the paper, dredge it witn flour, turn the spit
for some minutes very quick, and baste all
the time to raise a froth—after which, serve
it up. When mutton is roasted, after you
take off the paper, loosen the skin and peel
it off carefully, then dredge and froth it up.
Beef and mutton must not be roasted as much
as veal, lamb, or pork; the two last must be
skinned in the manner directed for mutton.—
You may pour a little melted butter in the
dish with veal, but all the others must be
served without sauce, and garnished with
horse-radish, nicely scraped. Be careful not
to let a particle of dry flour be seen on the
meat—it has a very ill appearance. Beef
may look brown, but the whiter the other
meats are, the more genteel are they, and if
properly roasted, they may be perfectly done,
and quite white. A loin of veal, and hind
quarter of lamb, should be dished with the
kidneys uppermost; and be sure to joint
every thing that is to be separated at table, or
it will be impossible to carve neatly. For

those who *must* have gravy with these meats, let it be made in any way they like, and served in a boat. No meat can be well roasted, except on a spit turned by a jack, and before a steady clear fire—other methods are no better than baking. Many cooks are in the habit of half-boiling the meats to plump then as they term it, before they are spitted, but it destroys their fine flavour. Whatever is to be boiled, must be put into cold water with a little salt, which will cook them regularly. When they are put in boiling water, the outer side is done too much before the inside gets heated. Nice lard is much better than butter for basting roasted meats, or for frying. To choose butcher's meat, you must see that the fat is not yellow, and that the lean parts are of a fine close grain, a lively colour, and will feel tender when pinched. Poultry should be well covered with white fat; if the bottom of the breast bone be gristly, it is young, but if it be a hard bone it is an old one. Fish are judged by the liveliness of their eyes, and bright red of their gills. If the weather should become close and damp, while there is a large supply

C

of provisions in the house, the best way to preserve them is to wash each piece in a quantity of cold water, wipe it perfectly dry with a cloth, and rub some dry bran over it, then hang it in the coolest place. This must be done every morning till the weather changes. Beef and mutton will keep much longer than veal, lamb, or pork. Poultry may be preserved in the same manner, by having a little mop to scour the inside, and another to wipe it dry; but as they are more difficult to keep than butcher's meat it would be best to dress them when there is much danger of their spoiling, and either eat them cold, or recook them some other way. Dredge every thing with flour before it is put on to boil, and be sure to add salt to the water.

Fish, and all other articles for frying, after being nicely prepared, should be laid on a board and dredged with flour or meal mixed with salt: when it becomes dry on one side, turn it, and dredge the other. For broiling, have very clear coals, sprinkle a little salt and pepper over the pieces, and when done, dish them, and pour over some melted butter and chopped parsley—this is for broiled veal.

wild fowl, birds, or poultry: Beef-steaks
and mutton chops require only a table-spoon-
full of hot water to be poured over. Slice
an-onion in the dish before you put in the
steaks or chops, and garnish both with rasped horse-radish. To have viands served in
perfection, the dishes should be made hot,
either by setting them over hot water, or by
putting some in them, and the instant the
meats are laid in and garnished, put on a
pewter dish cover. A dinner looks very
enticing, when the steam rises from each dish
on removing the covers, and if it be judicious-
ly *ordered*, will have a double relish. Profusion is not elegance—a dinner justly cal-
culated for the company, and consisting for
the greater part of small articles, correctly
prepared, and neatly served up, will make a
much more pleasing appearance to the sight,
and give a far greater gratification to the ap-
petite, than a table loaded with food, and
from the multiplicity of dishes, unavoidably
neglected in the preparation, and served up
cold.

There should always be a supply of brown
flour kept in readiness to thicken brown gra-

vies, which must be prepared in the following manner:—Put a pint of flour in a Dutch oven, with some coals under it; keep constantly stirring it until it is uniformly of a dark brown, but none of it burnt, which would look like dirt in the gravy. All kitchens should be provided with a saw for trimming meat, and also with larding needles.

TO MAKE BEEF SOUP.

Take the hind shin of beef, cut off all the flesh of the leg-bone, which must be taken away entirely, or the soup will be greasy.— Wash the meat clean and lay it in a pot, sprinkle over it one small table-spoonful of pounded black pepper, and two of salt; three onions the size of a hen's egg, cut small, six small carrots scraped and cut up, two small turnips pared and cut into dice; pour on three quarts of water, cover the pot close, and keep it gently and steadily boiling five hours, which will leave about three pints of clear soup; do not let the pot boil over, but take off the scum carefully, as it rises.— When it has boiled four hours, put in a small bundle of thyme and parsley, and a pint of celery cut small, or a tea-spoonful of celery seed pounded. These latter ingredients, would lose their delicate flavour if boiled too much. Just before you take it up brown it in the following manner:—Put a small table-spoonful of nice brown sugar into an iron skillet, set it on the fire and stir it till it melts and looks very dark, pour into it a ladle full of the soup, a little at a time stirring it all the while. Strain this browning and mix it well with the soup; take out the bundle of thyme and parsley, put the nicest pieces of meat in your tureen, and pour on the soup and vegetables, put in some toasted bread cut in dice, and serve it up.

TO MAKE GRAVY SOUP.

Get eight pounds of coarse lean beef— wash it clean and lay it in your pot, put in the same ingredients as for the shin soup, with the same quantity of water, and follow the process directed for that. Strain the soup through a seive and serve it up clear with nothing more than toasted bread

in it, two table-spoonsful of mushroom catsup will add a fine flavour to the soup.

SOUP WITH BOUILLI.

Take the nicest part of the thick brisket
of beef about eight pounds, put it into a
pot with every thing directed for the other
soup; make it exactly in the same way,
only put it on an hour sooner that you may
have time to prepare the bouilli, after it has
boiled five hours take out the beef, cover up
the soup and set it near the fire that it may
keep hot. Take the skin off the beef, have
the yelk of an egg well beaten, dip a feather
in it and wash the top of you beef, sprinkle
over it the crumb of stale bread finely grated,
put in a Dutch oven previously heated,
put the top on with coals enough to brown,
but not burn the beef; let it stand nearly
an hour and prepare your gravy thus :—
Take a sufficient quantity of soup and the
vegetables boiled in it; add to it a table-
spoonful of red wine, and two of mushroom catsup, thicken with a little bit of butter and a little brown flour: make it very

hot, pour it in your dish, and put the beef on
it. Garnish it with green pickle, cut in thin
slices, serve up the soup in a tureen with bits
of toasted bread.

———

VEAL SOUP.

Put into a pot three quarts of water, three
onions cut small, one spoonful of black pepper pounded, and two of salt, with two or
three slices of lean ham ; let it boil steadily
two hours ; skim it occasionally, then put
into it a shin of veal, let it boil two hours
longer; take out the slices of ham, and skim
off the grease if any should rise, take a gill
of good cream, mix with it two table-spoonsful of flour very nicely, and the yelks of
two eggs beaten well, strain this mixture,
and add some chopped parsley; pour some
soup on by degrees, stir it well, and pour it
into the pot continuing to stir until it has
boiled two or three minutes to take off the
raw taste of the eggs. If the cream be not
perfectly sweet, and the eggs quite new, the
thickening will curdle in the soup. For a
change, you may put a dozen ripe tomatas

in, first taking off their skins, by letting them stand a few minutes in hot water, when they may be easily peeled. When made in this way, you must thicken it with the flour only. Any part of the veal may be used, but the shin or knuckle is the nicest.

OYSTER SOUP.

Put on two quarts of oysters, with three quarts of water, three onions chopped up, two or three slices of lean ham, pepper and salt; boil it till reduced one half, strain it through a seive, return the liquid into the pot, put in one quart of fresh oysters, boil it till they are sufficiently done, and thicken the soup with four spoonsful of flour, two gills of rich cream, and the yelks of six new laid eggs beaten well; boil it a few minutes after the thickening is put in. Take care that it does not curdle, and that the flour is not in lumps: serve it up with the last oysters that were put in. If the flavour of thyme be agreeable you may put in a little, but take care that it does not boil in it long enough to discolour the soup.

BARLEY SOUP.

Put on three gills of barley, three quarts of water, a few onions cut up, six carrots, scraped and cut in dice, an equal quantity of turnips cut small: boil it gently two hours, then put in four or five pounds of the rack or neck of mutton, a few slices of lean ham, with pepper and salt ; boil it slowly, two hours longer, and serve it up. Tomatas are an excellent addition to this soup.

DRIED PEA SOUP.

Take one quart of split peas, or Lima beans which are better, put them in three quarts of very soft water with three onions chopped up, pepper and salt ; boil them two hours; wash them well and pass them through a seive ; return the liquid into the pot, thicken it with a large piece of butter and flour, put in some slices of nice salt pork, and a large tea-spoonful of celery-seed pounded; boil it till the pork is done, and serve it up; have some toasted bread cut into dice and fried in butter, which must be put in the tureen before you pour in the soup.

———

GREEN PEA SOUP.

Make it exactly as you do the dried pea soup, only in place of the celery-seed, put a handful of mint chopped small, and a pint of young peas which must be boiled in the soup till tender; thicken it with a quarter of a pound of butter, and two spoonsful of flour.

———

OCHRA SOUP.

Get two double handsful of young ochra, wash and slice it thin, add two onions chopped fine, put it into a gallon of water at a very early hour in an earthen pipkin, or very nice iron pot: it must be kept steadily simmering, but not boiling: put in pepper and salt. At 12 o'clock, put in a handful of Lima beans, at half past one o'clock, add three young cimlins cleaned and cut in small pieces, a fowl, or knuckle of veal, a bit of bacon or pork that has been boiled, and six tomatas, with the skin taken off when nearly done; thicken with a spoonful of butter, mixed with one of flour. Have rice boiled to eat with it.

HARE SOUP.

Cut up two hares, put them into a pot with a piece of bacon, two onions chopped, a bundle of thyme and parsley which must be taken out before the soup is thickened, add pepper, salt, pounded cloves, and mace, put in a sufficient quantity of water, stew it gently three hours, thicken with a large spoonful of butter, and one of brown flour with a glass of red wine; boil it a few minutes longer, and serve it up with the nicest parts of the hares. Squirrels make soup equally good, done the same way.

ONION SOUP.

Chop up twelve large onions, boil them in three quarts of milk and water equally mixed, put in a bit of veal or fowl, and a piece of bacon, with pepper and salt. When the onions are boiled to pulp, thicken it with a large spoonful of butter mixed with one of flour. Take out the meat, and serve it up with toasted bread cut in small pieces in the soup.

—

TO MAKE SOUP OF ANY KIND OF FOWL.

(The only way in which they are eatable.)

Put the fowls in a coop and feed them moderately for a fortnight; kill one and cleanse it, cut off the legs and wings, and separate the breast from the ribs; which, together with the whole back, must be thrown away, being too gross and strong for use. Take the skin and fat from the parts cut off which are also gross. Wash the pieces nicely and put them on the fire with about a pound of bacon, a large onion chopped small, some pepper and salt, a few blades of mace, a handful of parsley cut up very fine, and two quarts of water if it be a common fowl or duck—a turkey will require more water. Boil it gently for three hours, tie up a small bunch of thyme, and let it boil in it half an hour, then take it out. Thicken your soup with a large spoonful of butter rubbed into two of flour, the yelks of two eggs, and half-pint of milk. Be careful not to let it curdle in the soup.

———

TO MAKE CATFISH SOUP.

In excellent Dish for those who have not imbibed a needless prejudice against those delicious Fish.)

Take two large or four small white catfish that have been caught in deep water, cut off the heads, and skin and clean the bodies, cut each in three parts, put them in a pot with a pound of bacon, a large onion cut up, a handful of parsley chopped small, some pepper and salt, pour in a sufficient quantity of water, and stew them till the fish is quite tender and not broken, beat the yelks of four fresh eggs, add to them a large spoonful of butter, two of flour, and half a pint of rich milk, make all these warm and thicken the soup, take out the bacon, and put some of the fish in your tureen, pour in the soup, and serve it up.

———

ASPARAGUS SOUP.

Take four large bunches of asparagus,

D

scrape it nicely, cut off one inch of the tops, and lay them in water, chop the stalks and put them on the fire with a piece of bacon, a a large onion cut up, and pepper and salt; add two quarts water, boil them till the stalks are quite soft, then pulp them through a sieve, and strain the water to it, which must be put back in the pot; put into it a chicken cut up, with the tops of asparagus which had been laid by, boil it until these last articles are sufficiently done, thicken with flour, butter, and milk, and serve it up.

BEEF A-LA-MODE.

Take the bone from a round of beef, fill the space with a forcemeat made of the crumbs of a stale loaf, four ounces of marrow, two heads of garlic chopped with thyme and parsley, some nutmeg, cloves, pepper, and salt, mix it to a paste with the yelks of four eggs beaten, stuff the lean part of the round with it, and make balls of the remainder; sew a fillet of strong linen wide enough to keep it round and compact, put it in a vessel just sufficiently large to hold it, add a pint of red wine, cover it with sheets of tin or iron, set it in a brick oven properly neated, and bake it three hours; when done, skim the fat from the gravy, thicken it with brown flour, add some mushroom and walnut catsup, and serve it up garnished with forcemeat balls fried. It is still better when eaten cold with sallad.

BRISKET OF BEEF BAKED.

Bone a brisket of beef, and make holes in it with a sharp knife about an inch apart, fill them alternately with fat bacon, parsley, and oysters, all chopped small and seasoned with pounded cloves and nutmeg, pepper and salt, dredge it well with flour, lay it in a pan with a pint of red wine and a large spoonful of lemon pickle; bake it three hours, take the fat from the gravy and strain it; serve it up garnished with green pickles.

BEEF OLIVES.

Cut slices from a fat rump of beef six inch-

es long and half an inch thick, beat them well
with a pestle, make a forcemeat of bread
crumbs, fat bacon chopped, parsley, a little
onion, some shred suet, pounded mace, pepper and salt; mix it up with the yelks of eggs,
and spread a thin layer over each slice of
beef, roll it up tight and secure the rolls with
skewers, set them before the fire, and turn
them till they are a nice brown, have ready
a pint of good gravy thickened with brown
flour and a spoonful of butter, a gill of red
wine with two spoonsful of mushroom catsup, lay the rolls in it and stew them till tender: garnish with forcemeat balls.

TO STEW A RUMP OF BEEF.

Take out as much of the bone as can be
done with a saw, that it may lie flat in the
dish, stuff it with forcemeat made as before
directed, lay it in a pot with two quarts of
water, a pint of red wine, some carrots and
turnips cut in small pieces and strewed over
it, a head of cellery cut up, a few cloves of
garlic, some pounded cloves, pepper and salt,
stew it gently till sufficiently done, skim the fat

off, thicken the gravy and serve it up ; garnish with little bits of puff paste nicely baked, and scraped horse radish.

A FRICANDO OF BEEF.

Cut a few slices of beef six inches long, two or three wide, and one thick, lard them with bacon, dredge them well, and make them a nice brown before a brisk fire ; stir them half an hour in a well seasoned gravy, put some stewed sorrel or spinage in the dish, lay on the beef, and pour over a sufficient quantity of gravy ; garnish with fried balls.

AN EXCELLENT METHOD OF DRESSING BEEF.

Take a rib roasting piece that has been hanging ten days or a fortnight, bone it neatly, rub some salt over it and roll it tight, binding it around with twine, put the spit through the inner fold without sticking it in the flesh-skewer it well and roast it nicely ; when nearly done, dredge and froth it, garnish with scraped horse radish.

D 2

TO COLLAR A FLANK OF BEEF.

Get a nice flank of beef, rub it well with a large portion of salt petre and common salt, let it remain ten days, then wash it clean, take off the outer and inner skin with the gristle, spread it on a board and cover the inside with the following mixture : parsley, sage, thyme, chopped fine, pepper, salt, and pounded cloves, roll it up, sew a cloth over it and bandage that with tape, boil it gently five or six hours, when cold lay it on a board without undoing it, put another board on the top with a heavy weight on it, let it remain twenty-four hours, take off the bandages, cut a thin slice from each end, serve it up garnished with green pickle and sprigs of parsley.

TO MAKE HUNTER'S BEEF.

Select a fine fat round weighing about twenty-five pounds, take three ounces saltpetre, three of brown sugar, one ounce of cloves, half an ounce of alspice, a large nutmeg, and a quart of salt, pound them all together very fine, take the bone out, rub it well with this mixture on both sides, put some of it at the bottom of a tub just large enough to hold the beef, lay it in and strew the remainder on the top, rub it well every day for two weeks, and spread the mixture over it; at the end of this time wash the beef, bind it with tape to keep it round and compact, filling the hole where the bone was, with a piece of fat, lay it in a pan of convenient size, strew a little suet over the top and pour in a pint of water, cover the pan with a coarse crust and a thick paper over that, it will take five hours baking; when cold take off the tape. It is a delicious relish at twelve oclock, or for supper, eaten with vinegar, mustard, oil, or sallad. Skim the grease from the gravy and bottle it; it makes an excellent seasoning for any made dish.

A NICE LITTLE DISH OF BEEF.

Mince cold roast beef, fat and lean, very fine, add chopped onion, pepper, salt, and a little good gravy, fill scollop shells two parts full, and fill them up with potatoes mashed smooth with cream, put a bit of butter on the top, and set them in an oven to brown.

BEEF STEAKS.

The best part of the beef for steaks, is the seventh and eight ribs, the fat and lean are better mixed, and it is more tender than the rump if it be kept long enough ; cut the steaks half an inch thick, beat them a little, have fine clear coals, rub the bars of the gridiron with a cloth dipped in lard before you put it over the coals, that none may drip to cause a bad smell, put no salt on till you dish them, broil them quick, turning them frequently ; the dish must be very hot, put some slices of onion in it, lay in the steaks, sprinkle a little salt, and pour over them a spoonful of water and one of mushroom catsup, both made boiling hot, garnish with scraped horse radish, and put on a hot dish cover. Every thing must be in readiness, for the great excellence of a beaf steak lies in having it immediately from the gridiron.

TO HASH BEEF.

Cut slices of raw beef, put them in a stew pan with a little water, some catsup, a clove of garlic, pepper and salt, stew them till done, thicken the gravy with a lump of butter rubbed into brown flour. A hash may be made of any kind of meat that has been cooked, but it is not so good, and it is necessary to have a gravy prepared and seasoned, and keep the hash over the fire only a few minutes to make it hot.

———

BEEF STEAK PIE.

Cut nice steaks and stew them till half done, put a puff paste in the dish, lay in the steaks with a few slices of boiled ham, season the gravy very high, pour it in the dish, put on a lid of paste and bake it.

———

VEAL CUTLETS FROM THE FILLET OR LEG.

Cut off the flank and take the bone out, then take slices the size of the fillet and half an inch thick, beat two yelks of eggs light, and have some grated bread mixed with pepper, salt, pounded nutmeg and chopped parsley; beat the slices a little, lay them on a board and wash the upper side with the egg, cover it thick with the bread crumbs, press them on with a knife, and let them stand to dry a little, that they may not fall off in frying, then turn them gently, put egg and crumbs on in in the same manner, put them into a pan of boiling lard, and fry them a light brown ; have some good gravy ready, season it with a teaspoonful of curry powder, a large one of wine, and one of lemon pickle, thicken with butter and brown flour, drain every drop of lard from the cutlets, lay them in the gravy, and stew them fifteen or twenty minutes ; serve them up garnished with lemon cut in thin slices.

VEAL CHOPS.

Take the best end of a rack of veal, cut it in chops with one bone in each, leave the small end of the bone bare two inches, beat them flat, and prepare them with eggs and crumbs as the cutlets, butter some half-sheets of white paper, wrap one round each chop, skewer it well, leaving the bare bone out, broil them till done, and take care the paper does not burn ; have nice white sauce in a boat.

KNUCKLE OF VEAL.

Boil a half pint of pearl barley in salt and water till quite tender, drain the water from it and stir in a piece of butter, put it in a deep dish, have the knuckle nicely boiled in milk and water and lay it on the barley, pour some parsley and butter over it.

BAKED FILLET OF VEAL.

Take the bone out of the fillet, wrap the paper around and sew it, make a forcemeat of bread crumbs, the fat of bacon, a little onion chopped, parsley, pepper, salt, and a nutmeg pounded, wet it with the yelks of eggs, fill the place from which the bone was taken, make holes around it with a knife and fill them also, and lard the top, put it in a Dutch oven with a pint of water, bake it sufficiently, thicken the gravy with butter and brown flour, add a gill of wine and one of mushroom catsup, and serve it garnished with forcemeat balls fried.

SCOTCH COLLOPS OF VEAL.

They may be made of the nice part of the

rack, or cut from the fillet, rub a little salt and
pepper on them and fry them a light brown,
have a rich gravy seasoned with wine and
any kind of catsup you chuse, with a few
cloves of garlic and some pounded mace,
thicken it, put the collops in and stew them a
short time, take them out strain the gravy
over and garnish with bunches of parsley fried
crisp, and thin slices of middling of bacon
curled around a skewer and boiled.

VEAL OLIVES.

Take the bone out of the fillet and cut thin
slices the size of the leg, beat them flat, rub
them with the yelk of an egg beaten, lay on
each piece a thin slice of boiled ham, sprinkle salt, pepper, grated nutmeg, chopped parsley and bread crumbs over all, roll them up
tight and secure them with skewers, rub them
with egg and roll them in bread crumbs, lay
them on a tin dripping pan and set them in
an oven, when brown on one side turn them,
and when sufficiently done, lay them in a
rich highly seasoned gravy made of proper
thickness, stew them till tender, garnish with
forcemeat balls and green pickles sliced.

RAGOUT OF A BREAST OF VEAL.

Separate the joints of the brisket, and saw off the sharp ends of the ribs, trim it neatly and half roast it ; put it in a stew pan with a quart of good gravy seasoned with wine, walnut, and mushroom catsup, a tea-spoonful of curry powder and a few cloves of garlic, stew it till tender, thicken the gravy and garnish with sweet breads nicely broiled.

FRICANDO OF VEAL.

Cut slices from the fillet an inch thick and six inches long, lard them with slips of lean middling of bacon, bake them a light brown, stew them in well seasoned gravy, made as thick as rich cream, serve them up hot and lay round the dish sorrel stewed with butter, pepper, and salt, till quite dry.

A loin of veal must always be roasted ; the fillet or leg may be dressed in various ways, the knuckle or knee is proper for soup or for boiling ; these are the pieces that compose the hind quarter. In the fore quarter, the breast and rack admit variety in cooking ; the shoulder and neck are only fit for soup.

E

MOCK TURTLE OF CALF'S HEAD.

Have the head nicely cleaned, divide the chop from the scull, take out the brains and tongue, and boil the other parts till tender, take them out of the water and put into it a knuckle of veal or four pounds of lean beef, three onions chopped, thyme, parsley, a tea-spoonful of pounded cloves, the same of mace; salt, and cayenne pepper, to your taste, boil these things together till reduced to a pint, strain it and add two gills of red wine, one of mushroom and one of walnut catsup, thicken it with butter and brown flour; the head must be cut in small pieces and stewed a few minutes in the gravy; put a paste round the edge of a deep dish, three folds one on the other, but none on the bottom, pour in the meat and gravy, and bake it till the paste is done; pick all strings from the brains, pound them, and add grated bread, pepper, and salt, make them in little cakes with the yelk of an egg, fry them a nice brown, boil six eggs hard, leave one whole and divide the others exact-ly in two, have some bits of paste nicely baked; when the head is taken from the oven, lay the whole egg in the middle, and dispose

the others, with the brain cakes and bits of
paste, tastily around it. If it be wanted as
soup, do not reduce the gravy so much, and
after stewing the head, serve it in a tureen
with the brain cakes and forcemeat balls fried,
in place of the eggs and paste. The tongue
should be salted and put in brine ; they are
very delicate, and four of them boiled and
pealed, and served with four small chickens
boiled, make a handsome dish, either cold or
hot, with parsley and butter poured over them.

TO GRILL A CALF'S HEAD.

Clean and divide it as for the turtle, take
out the brains and tongue, boil it tender, take
the eyes out whole, and cut the flesh from
the scull in small pieces ; take some of the
water it was boiled in for gravy, put to it
salt, cayenne pepper, a grated nutmeg, with a
spoonful of lemon pickle ; stew it till it is well
flavoured, take the jowl or chop, do not take
out the bone, but saw off the lower part with
the teeth, cover it with bread crumbs, chopped parsley, pepper and salt, set it in an oven
to brown, thicken the gravy with the yelks

of two eggs and a spoonful of butter rubbed into two of flour, stew the head in it a few minutes, put it in the dish, and lay the grilled chop on it; garnish it with brain cakes and broiled sweet breads.

TO COLLAR A CALF'S-HEAD.

After cleaning it nicely, saw the bone down the middle of the scull, but do not separate the head, take out the brains and tongue, boil it tender enough to remove the bones, which must be taken entirely out; lay it on a board, have a good quantity of chopped parsley seasoned with mace, nutmeg, pepper, and salt, spread a layer of this, then one of thick slices of ham, another of parsley and one of ham, roll it up tight, sew a cloth over it and bind that round with tape, boil it half an hour and when cold press it; it must be kept covered with vinegar and water, and is very delicious eaten with sallad or oil and vinegar.

CALF'S HEART, A NICE DISH.

Take the heart and liver from the harslet and cut off the windpipe, boil the lights very tender, and cut them in small pieces, take as much of the water they were boiled in as will be sufficient for gravy, add to it a large spoonful of white wine, one of lemon pickle, some grated nutmeg, pepper, and salt, with a large spoonful of butter mixed with one of white flour, let it boil a few minutes and put in the minced lights, set it by till the heart and liver are ready, cut the ventricle out of the heart, wash it well, lard it all over with narrow slips of middling, fill the cavity with good forcemeat, put it in a pan on the broad end that the stuffing may not come out, bake it a nice brown, slice the liver an inch thick and broil it, make the mince hot, set the heart upright in the middle of the dish, pour it around, lay the broiled liver on, and garnish with bunches of fried parsley ; it should be served up extremely hot.

———

CALF'S FEET FRICASSEE.

Boil the feet till very tender, cut them in two and pull out the large bones, have half a pint of good white gravy, add to it a spoonful of white wine, one of lemon pickle, and some salt with a teaspoonful of curry powder, stew the feet in it fifteen minutes, and thicken it with the yelks of two eggs, a gill of milk, a large spoonful of butter, and two of white flour, let the thickening be very smooth, shake the stewpan over the fire a few minutes, but do not let it boil lest the eggs and milk should curdle.

———

TO FRY CALF'S FEET.

Prepare them as for the fricassee, dredge them well with flour and fry them a light brown, pour parsley and butter over and garnish with fried parsley.

Directions for cleaning calve's head and feet, for those who live in the country and butcher their own meats. As soon as the animal is killed, have the head and feet taken off, wash them clean, sprinkle some pounded rosin all over the hairs, then dip them in boiling water, take them instantly out, the rosin will dry immediately, and they may be scraped clean with ease, the feet should be soaked in water three or four days, changing it daily, this will make them very white.

TO MAKE A PIE OF SWEETBREADS AND OYSTERS.

Boil the sweetbreads tender, stew the oysters, season them with pepper and salt, and thicken with cream, butter, the yelks of eggs and flour, put a puff paste at the bottom and around the sides of a deep dish, take the oysters up with an egg spoon, lay them in the bottom and cover them with the sweetbreads, fill the dish with the gravy, put a paste on the top and bake it. This is the most delicious pie that can be made. The sweetbread of veal is the most delicious part, and may be broiled, fried, or dressed in any way, and is always good.

TO PREPARE THE STOMACH OF THE CALF FOR RENNET.

As soon as it is taken out cut it open lengthway, empty it of its contents and wash it in several changes of warm water, rub it with salt and let it remain two or three days, then wash it, stretch it on slender sticks and dry it in the shade ; when as dry as parchment, which it will resemble, put it in paper bags and keep it in a dry place. it will remain good two years.

LAMB.

The fore quarter should always be roasted and served with mint sauce in a boat, chop the mint small and mix it with vinegar enough to make it liquid, sweeten it with sugar.

The hind quarter may be boiled or roasted, and requires mint sauce ; it may also be dressed in various ways.

—

BAKED LAMB.

Cut the shank bone from a hind quarter, separate the joints of the loin, lay it in a pan with the kidney uppermost, sprinkle some pepper and salt, add a few cloves of garlic, a pint of water and a dozen large ripe tomatas with the skins taken off, bake it but do not let it be burnt, thicken the gravy with a little butter and brown flour.

—

FRIED LAMB.

Separate the leg from the loin, cut off the shank and boil the leg ; divide the loin in chops, dredge and fry them a nice brown, lay the leg in the middle of the dish and put the chops around, pour over parsley and butter, and garnish with fried parsley.

The leg cut into steaks and the loin into chops will make a fine fricassee, or cutlets.

———

TO DRESS LAMB'S HEAD AND FEET.

Clean them very nicely, and boil them till tender, take off the flesh from the head with the eyes, also mince the tongue and heart which must be boiled with the head, split the feet in two, put them with the pieces from the head and the mince, into a pint of good gravy seasoned with pepper, salt, and tomata catsup, or ripe tomatas, stew it till tender, thicken the gravy and lay the liver cut in slices and broiled over it ; garnish with crisp parsley and bits of curled bacon.

———

MUTTON.

The saddle should always be roasted and garnished with scraped horse raddish. See general observations on roasting. Mutton is in the highest perfection from August until Christmas, when it begins to decline in goodness.

BOILED LEG OF MUTTON.

Cut off the shank, wrap the flank nicely
round and secure it with skewers, dredge it
well with flour, and put it on the fire in a kettle
of cold water with some salt and three or four
heads of garlic, which will give it a delicately
fine flavour; skim it well and when nearly done
take it from the fire and keep it hot and closely covered, that the steam may finish it ; have
carrots well boiled to put in the dish under it,
or turnips boiled, mashed smooth and stewed
with a lump of butter and salt, lay the mutton on, and pour over it, butter melted with
some flour in it, and a cup full of capers with
some of the vinegar ; shake them together
over the fire till hot before you pour it on.

ROASTED LEG.

Prepare it as for boiling, be very careful
in spitting it, cover it with paper and follow
the directions for roasting, serve it up garnished with scraped horse raddish.

BAKED LEG OF MUTTON.

Take the flank off but leave all the fat, cut

out the bone, stuff the place with a rich forcemeat, lard the top and sides with bacon, put
it in a pan with a pint of water, some chopped
onion and cellery cut small, a gill of red wine,
one of mushroom catsup and a teaspoonful of
curry powder, bake it and serve it up with the
gravy, garnish with forcemeat balls fried.

STEAKS OF A LEG OF MUTTON.

Cut off the flank, take out the bone, and
cut it in large slices half an inch thick, sprinkle some salt and pepper and broil it, pour
over it nice melted butter with capers; a leg
cut in the same way and dressed as directed
for veal cutlets is very fine. It is also excellent when salted as beef, and boiled, served
up with carrots or turnips.

A shoulder of mutton is best when roasted,
but may be made into cutlets or in a harrico.

TO HARRICO MUTTON.

Take the nicest part of the rack, divide it
into chops with one bone in each, beat them
flat, sprinkle salt and pepper on them, and
broil them nicely; make a rich gravy out of

the inferior parts, season it well with pepper, a little spice, and any kind of catsup you chuse ; when sufficiently done, strain it and thicken it with butter and brown flour, have some carrots and turnips cut into small dice and boiled till tender, put them in the gravy, lay the chops in and stew them fifteen minutes; serve them up garnished with green pickle.

MUTTON CHOPS.

Cut the rack as for the harrico, broil them, and when dished, pour over them a gravy made with two large spoonsful of boiling water, one of mushroom catsup, a small spoonful of butter and some salt, stir it till the butter is melted, and garnish with horse-radish scraped.

BOILED BREAST OF MUTTON.

Separate the joints of the brisket, and saw off the sharp ends of the ribs, dredge it with flour, and boil it ; serve it up covered with onions—see onion sauce.

BREAST OF MUTTON IN RAGOUT.

Prepare the breast as for broiling, brown

it nicely in the oven, have a rich gravy well seasoned and thickened with brown flour, stew the mutton in it till sufficiently done, and garnish with forcemeat balls fried.

TO GRILL A BREAST OF MUTTON.

Prepare it as before, score the top, wash it over with the yelk of an egg, sprinkle some salt, and cover it with bread crumbs, bake it and pour caper sauce in the dish. It may also be roasted, the skin taken off and frothed nicely, serve it up with good gravy, and garnish with currant jelly cut in slices.

The neck of mutton is fit only for soup; the liver is very good when broiled.

BOILED SHOULDER OF MUTTON.

Put it in cold water with some salt, and boil it till tender; serve it up covered with onion sauce.

SHOULDER OF MUTTON WITH CELERY SAUCE.

Wash and clean ten heads of celery, cut off the green tops and take off the outside stalks, cut the heads in thin slices, boil them tender in a little milk, just enough for gravy,

F

add salt, and thicken it with a spoonful of butter and some white flour; boil the shoulder and pour the sauce over it.

___

ROASTED LOIN OF MUTTON.

Cut the loin in four pieces, take off the skin, rub each piece with salt, wash them with the yelk of an egg, and cover them thickly with bread crumbs, chopped parsley, pepper and salt; wrap them up securely in paper, put them on a bird spit, and roast them; put a little brown gravy in the dish, and garnish with pickle.

___

PORK.—TO ROAST A PIG.

The pig must be very fat, nicely cleaned, and not too large to lie in the dish; chop the liver fine and mix it with crumbs of bread, chopped onion and parsley, with pepper and salt, make it into a paste with butter and an egg, stuff the body well with it and sew it up, spit it and have a clear fire to roast it; baste with salt and water at first, then rub it frequently with a lump of lard wrapped in a piece of clean Linen; this will make it much more crisp than basting it from the dripping pan. When the pig is done, take off the head, separate the face from the chop, cut both in two and take off the ears, take out the suffing, split the pig in two parts lengthway, lay it in the dish with the head, ears, and feet, which have been cut off, placed on each side, put the stuffing in a bowl with a glass of wine and as much dripping as will make it sufficiently liquid, put some of it under the pig, and serve the rest in a boat.

TO BARBECUE SHOTE.

This is the name given in the southern states to a fat young hog, which, when the head and feet are taken off, and it is cut into four quarters, will weigh six pounds per quarter. Take a fore quarter, make several incisions between the ribs, and stuff it with rich forcemeat; put it in a pan with a pint of water, two cloves garlic, pepper, salt, two gills of red wine, and two of mushroom catsup, bake it and thicken the gravy with butter and brown flour; it must be jointed and the ribs cut across before it is cooked, or it cannot be carved well; lay it in the dish with the ribs uppermost; if it be not sufficiently brown, add a little sugar to the gravy; garnish with balls.

TO ROAST A FORE QUARTER OF SHOTE.

Joint it for the convenience of carving, roast it before a brisk fire ; when done, take the skin off, dredge and froth it, put a little melted butter with some caper vinegar over it, or serve it with mint sauce.

TO MAKE SHOTE CUTLETS.

Take the skin from the hind quarter, and cut it in pieces, prepare them in the way directed for veal cutlets, make a little nice gravy with the skin and the scraps of meat left, thicken it with butter and brown flour, and season it in any way you like.

TO CORN SHOTE.

Rub a hind quarter with salt petre and common salt, let it lie ten days, then boil it, and put either carrots or parsneps under it.

SHOTE'S HEAD.

Take out the brains and boil the head till quite tender, cut the heart and liver from the harslet, and boil the feet with the head ; cut all the meat from the head in small pieces, mince the tongue and chop the brains small, take some of the water the head was boiled

in, season it with onion, parsley, and thyme,
all chopped fine, add any kind of catsup,
thicken it with butter and brown flour, stew
the whole in it fifteen minutes, and put it in
the dish; have the heart roasted to put in the
middle, lay the broiled liver around, and garnish it with green pickle.

LEG OF PORK WITH PEASE PUDDING.

Boil a small leg of pork that has been sufficiently salted, score the top and serve it up;
the pudding must be in a separate dish; get
small delicate peas, wash them well, and tie
them in a cloth, allowing a little room for
swelling, boil them with the pork, then mash
and season them, tie them up again and finish
boiling it; take care not to break the pudding
in turning it out.

STEWED CHINE.

Take the neck chine, rub it well with salt,
lay it in a pan, put it in a pint of water, and
fill it up with sweet potatoes nicely washed,
but not peeled, cover it close and bake it till
done; serve it up with the potatoes, put a little of the gravy in the dish.

F 2

TO TOAST A HAM.

Boil it well, take off the skin, and cover the top thickly with bread crumbs, put it in an oven to brown, and serve it up.

TO STUFF A HAM.

Take a well smoked ham, wash it very clean, make incisions all over the top two inches deep, stuff them quite full with parsley chopped small and some pepper, boil the ham sufficiently; do not take off the skin. It must be eaten cold.

SOUSED FEET IN RAGOUT.

Split the feet in two, dredge them with flour and fry them a nice brown ; have some well seasoned gravy thickened with brown flour and butter, stew the feet in it a few minutes.

TO MAKE SAUSAGES.

Take the tender pieces of fresh pork, chop them exceedingly fine, chop some of the leaf fat, and put them together in the proportion of three pounds of pork to one of fat, season it very high with pepper and salt, add a small quantity of dried sage rubbed to a powder, have the skins nicely prepared, fill them and hang them in a dry place. Sausages are excellent made into cakes and fried, but will not keep so well as in skins.

TO MAKE BLACK PUDDINGS.

Catch the blood as it runs from the hog, stir it continually till cold to prevent its coagulating, when cold thicken it with boiled rice or oatmeal, add leaf fat chopped small, pepper, salt and any herbs that are liked, fill the skins and smoke them two or three days; they must be boiled before they are hung up, and prick them with a fork to keep them from bursting.

TO BAKE STURGEON.

Get a piece of sturgeon with the skin on the piece next to the tail, scrape it well, cut out the gristle, and boil it about twenty minutes to take out the oil; take it up, pull off the large scales, and when cold, stuff it with forcemeat, made of bread crumbs, butter, chopped parsley, pepper and salt, put it in a dutch oven just large enough to hold it, with a pint and a half of water, a gill of red wine, one of mushroom catsup, some salt and pepper, stew it gently till the gravy is reduced to the quantity necessary to pour over it; take up your sturgeon carefully, thicken the gravy with a spoonful of butter rubbed into a large one of brown flour; see that it is perfectly smooth when you put it in the dish.

TO MAKE STURGEON CUTLETS.

The tail piece is the best; skin it and cut off the gristle, cut it into slices about half an inch thick, sprinkle over them pepper and salt, dredge them with flour, and fry them a nice light brown; have ready a pint of good gravy, seasoned with catsup, wine, and a little pounded cloves, and thickened with brown flour and butter; when the cutlets are cold, put them into the gravy and stew them a few minutes; garnish the dish with nice force-meat balls and parsley fried crisp.

STURGEON STEAKS.

Cut them as for the cutlets, dredge them, and fry them nicely; dish them quickly lest they get cold, pour over melted butter with chopped parsley, and garnish with fried parsley.

TO BOIL STURGEON.

Leave the skin on, which must be nicely scraped, take out the gristle, rub it with salt and let it lie an hour, then put it on in cold water with some salt and a few cloves of garlic; it must be dredged with flour before it is put into the water, skim it carefully, and when dished, pour over it melted butter with chopped parsley, a large spoonful of mushroom catsup, one of lemon pickle, and one of pepper vinegar; send some of it to table in a sauce boat; the sturgeon being a dry fish, rich sauce is necessary.

———

TO BAKE A SHAD.

The shad is a very indifferent fish unless it be large and fat; when you get a good one prepare it nicely, put some force meat inside and lay it at full length in a pan, with a pint of water, a gill of red wine, one of mushroom catsup, a little pepper, vinegar, salt, a few cloves of garlic, and six cloves; stew it gently till the gravy is sufficiently reduced; there should always be a fish-slice with holes to lay the fish on, for the convenience of dishing without breaking it; when the fish is taken up, slip it carefully into the dish : thicken the gravy with butter and brown flour, and pour over it.

TO BOIL A SHAD.

Get a nice fat shad, fresh from the water, that the skin may not crack in boiling, put it in cold water on a slice, in a kettle of proper length, with a wine glass of pale vinegar, salt, a little garlic, and a bundle of parsley ; when it is done, drain all the water from the fish, lay it in the dish, and garnish with scraped horse radish ; have a sauce boat of nice melted butter, to mix with the different catsups as taste shall direct.

TO ROAST A SHAD.

Fill the cavity with good forcemeat, sew it up and tie it on a board of proper size, cover it with bread crumbs, with some salt and pepper, set it before the fire to roast ; when done on one side, turn it, tie it again, and when sufficiently done, pull out the thread, and serve it up with butter and parsley poured over it.

TO BROIL A SHAD.

Separate one side from the backbone, so that it will lie open without being split in two, wash it clean, dry it with a cloth, sprinkle some salt and pepper on it, and let it stand till you are ready to broil it; have the gridiron hot and well greased, broil it nicely, and pour over it melted butter.

TO BOIL ROCK FISH.

The best part of the rock is the head and shoulders; clean it nicely, put it into the fish kettle with cold water and salt, boil it gently and skim it well; when done, drain off the water, lay it in the dish, and garnish with scraped horse radish; have two boats of butter nicely melted with chopped parsley, or, for a change, you may have anchovy butter; the roe and liver should be fried and served in separate dishes. If any of the rock be left it will make a delicious dish next day; pick it in small pieces, put it in a stew pan with a gill of water, a good lump of butter, some salt, a large spoonful of lemon pickle and one of pepper vinegar, shake it over the fire till perfectly hot, and serve it up. It is almost equal to stewed crab.

TO FRY PERCH.

Clean the fish nicely, but do not take out the roes, dry them on a cloth, sprinkle some salt, and dredge them with flour, lay them separately on a board, when one side is dry, turn them, sprinkle salt and dredge the other side ; be sure the lard boils when you put the fish in and fry them with great care ; they should be a yellowish brown when done. Send melted butter or anchovy sauce in a boat.

TO PICKLE OYSTERS.

Select the largest oysters, drain off their liquor, and wash them in clean water ; pick out the pieces of shells that may be left, put them in a stew pan with water proportioned to the number of oysters, some salt, blades of mace, and whole black pepper ; stew them a few minutes, then put them in a pot, and when cold, add as much pale vinegar as will give the liquor an agreeable acid.

TO MAKE A CURRY OF CATFISH.

Take the white channel catfish, cut off their heads, skin and clean them, cut them in pieces four inches long, put as many as will be sufficient for a dish into a stew pan with a quart of water, two onions, and chopped parsley ; let them stew gently till the water is reduced to half a pint, take the fish out and lay them on a dish, cover them to keep them hot, rub a spoonful of butter into one of flour, add a large tea-spoonful of curry powder, thicken the gravy with it, shake it over the fire a few minutes, and pour it over the fish ; be careful to have the gravy smooth.

TO DRESS A COD'S HEAD AND SHOULDERS.

Take out the gills and the blood from the bone, wash the head very clean, rub over it a little salt, then lay it on your fish plate ; throw in the water a good handful of salt, with a glass of vinegar, then put in the fish, and let it boil gently half an hour ; if it is a large one, three quarters; take it up very carefully, strip the skin nicely off, set it before a brisk fire, dredge it all over with flour, and baste it well with butter ; when the froth begins to rise, throw over it some very fine white bread crumbs ; you must keep basting it all the time to make it froth well ; when it is a fine light brown, dish it up, and garnish it with a

G

lemon cut in slices, scraped horse radish, barberries, a few small fish fried and laid round
it, or fried oysters, cut the roe and liver in
slices, and lay over it a little of the lobster out
of the sauce in lumps, and then serve it up.

TO MAKE SAUCE FOR THE COD'S HEAD.

Take a lobster, if it be alive, stick a skewer
in the vent of the tail, (to keep the water out,)
throw a handful of salt in the water; when it
boils, put in the lobster and boil it half an
hour; if it has spawn on it, pick them off, and
pound them exceedingly fine in a marble
mortar, and put them into half a pound of
good melted butter, then take the meat out of
the lobster, pull it in bits and put it in your butter, with a meat spoonful of lemon pickle, and
the same of walnut catsup, a slice of lemon,
one or two slices of horse radish, a little beat-
en mace, salt and cayenne to your taste, boil
them one minute, then take out the horse radish and lemon, and serve it up in your sauce
boat.

N. B. if you cannot get lobsters, you may
make shrimp, cockle, or muscle sauce the
same way; if there can be no shell fish got,

you then may add two anchovies cut small,
a spoonful of walnut liquor, a large onion stuck
with cloves, strain and put it in the sauce boat.

TO DRESS A SALT COD.

Steep your salt fish in water all night, with
a glass of vinegar ; it will take out the salt,
and make it taste like fresh fish ; the next day
boil it ; when it is enough, take off the skin,
pull it in fleaks into your dish, then pour egg
sauce over it, or parsnips boiled and beat fine,
with butter and cream ; send it to the table
on a water plate, for it will soon grow cold.

TO MAKE EGG SAUCE FOR A SALT COD.

Boil four eggs hard, first half chop the
white, then put in the yelks and chop them
both together, but not very small, put them
into half a pound of good melted butter, and
let it boil up, then pour it on the fish.

TO DRESS COD SOUNDS.

Steep your sounds as you do the salt cod,
and boil them in a large quantity of milk and
water ; when they are very tender and white,
take them up, and drain the water out and

skin them, then pour the egg sauce boiling
hot over them and serve them up.

———

TO STEW CARP.

Gut and scale your fish, wash and dry
them well with a clean cloth, dredge them
with flour, fry them in lard until they are a
light brown, and then put them in a stew pan
with a pint of water and one pint of red wine,
a meat spoonful of lemon pickle, the same of
walnut catsup, a little mushroom powder and
cayenne to your taste, a large onion stuck
with cloves, and a stick of horse radish; cover your pan close up to keep in the steam,
let them stew gently over a stove fire till the
gravy is reduced to just enough to cover your
fish in the dish, then take the fish out and put
them on the dish you intend for the table;
set the gravy on the fire, and thicken it with
flour and a large lump of butter, boil it a little, and strain it over your fish; garnish them
with pickled mushrooms and scraped horse
radish, and send them to the table.

———

TO BOIL EELS.

Clean the eels and cut off their heads, dry

them and turn them round on your fish plate,
boil them in salt and water, and make parsley sauce for them.

TO PITCH-COCK EELS.

Skin and wash your eels, then dry them
with a cloth, sprinkle them with pepper, salt,
and a little dried sage, turn them backward
and forward, and skewer them; rub a gridiron with beef suet, broil them a nice brown,
put them on a dish with good melted butter,
and lay around fried parsley.

TO BROIL EELS.

When you have skinned and cleansed your
eels as before, rub them with the yelk of an
egg, strew over them bread crumbs, chopped
parsley, sage, pepper, and salt; baste them
well with butter, and set them in a dripping
pan; serve them up with parsley and butter
for sauce.

TO SCOLLOP OYSTERS.

When the oysters are opened, put them in
a bowl and wash them out of their own liquor, put some in the scollop shells, strew

over them a few bread crumbs, and lay a
slice of butter on them, then more oysters,
bread crumbs, and a slice of butter on the
top; put them into a dutch oven to brown,
and serve them up in the shells.

TO FRY OYSTERS.

Take a quarter of a hundred of large oysters, beat the yelks of two eggs, add to it a
little nutmeg and a blade of mace pounded, a
spoonful of flour, and a little salt; dip in the
oysters and fry them a light brown; if you
choose you may add a little parsley shred fine.
They are a proper garnish for calveshead, or
most made dishes.

TO MAKE OYSTER LOAVES.

Take little round loaves, cut off the top,
scrape out all the crumbs, then put the oysters
into a stew pan with the crumbs that came
out of the loaves, a little water, and a good
lump of butter; stew them together ten or fifteen minutes, then put in a spoonful of good
cream, fill your loaves, lay the bit of crust
carefully on again, set them in the oven to
crisp. Three are enough for a side dish.

TO ROAST A GOOSE.

Chop a few sage leaves and two onions very fine, mix them with a good lump of butter,
a teaspoonful of pepper and two of salt, put
it in the goose, then spit it, lay it down, and
dust it with flour ; when it is thoroughly hot,
baste it with nice lard; if it be a large one,
it will require an hour and a half, before a
good clear fire ; when it is enough, dredge
and baste it, pull out the spit, and pour in a
little boiling water.

TO MAKE SAUCE FOR A GOOSE.

Pare, core, and slice some apples, put them
in a sauce pan, with as much water as will
keep them from burning, set them over a very slow fire, keep them close covered till reduced to a pulp, then put in a lump of butter,
and sugar to your taste, beat them well, and
send them to the table in a china bowl.

TO BOIL DUCKS WITH ONION SAUCE.

Scald and draw your ducks, put them in
warm water for a few minutes, then take
them out and put them in an earthen pot ;
pour over them a pint of boiling milk, and let

them lie in it two or three hours; when you take them out, dredge them well with flour, and put them in a copper of cold water; put on the cover, let them boil slowly twenty minutes, then take them out and smother them with onion sauce.

TO MAKE ONION SAUCE.

Boil eight or ten large onions, change the water two or three times while they are boiling, when enough, chop them on a board to keep them a good colour, put them in a sauce pan with a quarter of a pound of butter and two spoonsful of thick cream, boil it a little, and pour it over the ducks.

TO ROAST DUCKS.

When you have drawn the ducks, shread one onion and a few sage leaves, put them into the ducks with pepper and salt, spit and dust them with flour, and baste them with lard: if your fire be very hot, they will roast in twenty minutes, and the quicker they are roasted the better they will taste; just before you draw them, dust them with flour, and baste them. Get ready some gravy made of the gizzards and pinions, a large blade of mace, a few pepper corns, a spoonful of catsup, and a tea-spoonful of lemon pickle; strain it and pour it on the ducks, and send onion sauce in a boat.

TO BOIL A TURKEY WITH OYSTER SAUCE.

Grate a loaf of bread, chop a score or more of oysters fine, add nutmeg pepper and salt to your taste, mix it up into a light forcemeat with a quarter of a pound of butter, a spoonful or two of cream, and three eggs; stuff the craw with it, and make the rest into balls and boil them; sew up the turkey, dredge it well with flour, put it in a kettle of cold water, cover it, and set it over the fire; as the scum begins to rise, take it off, let it boil very slowly for half an hour, then take off your kettle and keep it close covered; if it be of a middle size, let it stand in the hot water half an hour, the steam being kept in will stew it enough, make it rise, keep the skin whole, tender, and very white; when you dish it, pour on a little oyster sauce, lay the balls round, and serve it up with the rest of the sauce in a boat.

N. B. Set on the turkey in time, that it may stew as above ; it is the best way to boil one to perfection. Put it over the fire to heat, just before you dish it up.

TO MAKE SAUCE FOR A TURKEY.

As you open the oysters, put a pint into a bowl, wash them out of their own liquor, and put them in another bowl ; when the liquor has settled, pour it off into a sauce pan, with a little white gravy and a teaspoonful of lemon pickle, thicken it with flour and a good lump of butter, boil it three or four minutes, put in a spoonful of good cream, add the oysters, keep shaking them over the fire till they are quite hot, but don't let them boil, for it will make them hard and appear small.

TO ROAST A TURKEY.

Make the forcemeat thus : take the crumbs of a loaf of bread, a quarter of a pound of beef suet shread fine, a little sausage meat or veal scraped and pounded very fine, nutmeg, pepper, and salt to your taste, mix it lightly with three eggs, stuff the craw with it, spit it, and lay it down a good distance from the fire.

which should be clear and brisk, dust and baste it several times with cold lard, it makes the froth stronger than basting it with the hot out of the dripping pan, and makes the turkey rise better ; when it is enough, froth it up as before, dish it and pour on the same gravy as for the boiled turkey, or bread sauce ; garnish with lemon and pickles, and serve it up ; if it be of a middle size, it will require one hour and a quarter to roast.

TO MAKE SAUCE FOR A TURKEY.

Cut the crumb of a loaf of bread in thin slices and put it in cold water, with a few pepper corns, a little salt and onion, then boil it till the bread is quite soft, beat it well, put in a quarter of a pound of butter, two spoonsful of thick cream, and put it in a bowl.

TO BOIL FOWLS.

Dust the fowls well with flour, put them in a kettle of cold water, cover it close, set it on the fire ; when the scum begins to rise, take it off, let them boil very slowly for twenty minutes, then take them off, cover them close, and the heat of the water will stew them enough in half an hour; it keeps the skin whole, and they will be both whiter and plumper than if they had boiled fast; when you take them up, drain them, and pour over them white sauce or melted butter.

TO MAKE WHITE SAUCE FOR FOWLS.

Take a scrag of veal, the necks of fowls, or any bits of mutton or veal you have, put them in a sauce pan with a blade or two of mace, a few black pepper corns, one anchovy, a head of celery, a bunch of sweet herbs, a slice of the end of a lemon, put in a quart of water, cover it close, let it boil till it is reduced to half a pint, strain it, and thicken it with a quarter of a pound of butter mixed with flour, boil it five or six minutes, put in two spoonsful of pickled mushrooms, mix the yelks of two eggs with a tea cup full of good cream and a little nutmeg, put it in the sauce, keep shaking it over the fire but don't let it boil.

TO ROAST LARGE FOWLS.

Take the fowls when they are ready dressed, put them down to a good fire, dredge and baste them well with lard; they will be near an hour in roasting; make a gravy of the necks and gizards, strain it, put in a spoonful of brown flour; when you dish them, pour on the gravy, and serve them up with egg sauce in a boat.

TO MAKE EGG SAUCE.

Boil four eggs for ten minutes, chop half the whites, put them with the yelks, and chop them both together, but not very fine, put them into a quarter of a pound of good melted butter, and put it in a boat.

TO BOIL YOUNG CHICKENS.

Put the chickens in scalding water; as soon as the feathers will slip off, take them out, or it will make the skin hard and break; when you have drawn them, lay them in skimmed milk for two hours, then truss and dust them well with flour, put them in cold water, cover them close, set them over a very slow fire, take off the scum, let them boil slowly for five or six minutes, take them off the fire, keep them close covered in the water for half an hour, it will stew them enough: when you

H

are going to dish them, set them over the fire to make them hot, drain them, and pour over white sauce made the same way as for the boiled fowls.

TO ROAST YOUNG CHICKENS.

When you kill young chickens, pluck them very carefully, truss and put them down to a good fire, dredge and baste them with lard; they will take a quarter of an hour in roasting; froth them up, lay them on the dish, pour butter and parsley on, and serve them up hot.

TO ROAST WOODCOCKS OR SNIPES.

Pluck, but don't draw them, put them on a small spit, dredge and baste them well with lard, toast a few slices of bread, put them on a clean plate, and set it under the birds while they are roasting; if the fire be good, they will take about ten minutes; when you draw them, lay them upon the toasts on the dish, pour melted butter round them, and serve them up

TO ROAST WILD DUCKS OR TEAL.

When the ducks are ready dressed, put

in them a small onion, pepper, salt, and a spoonful of red wine; if the fire be good, they will roast in twenty minutes; make gravy of the necks and gizzards, a spoonful of red wine, half an anchovy, a blade or two of mace, one onion, and a little cayenne pepper, boil it till it is wasted to half a pint, strain it strough a hair sieve, and pour it on the ducks; serve them up with onion sauce in a boat; garnish the dish with raspings of bread.

TO BOIL PIGEONS.

Scald the pigeons, draw them, take the craw out, wash them in several waters, cut off the pinions, turn the legs under the wings, dredge them, and put them in soft cold water, boil them slowly a quarter of an hour, dish them up, pour over them good melted butter, lay round a little brocoli in bunches, and send butter and parsley in a boat.

TO ROAST PIGEONS.

When you have dressed your pigeons as before, roll a good lump of butter in chopped parsley, with pepper and salt, put it in your pigeons, spit, dust and baste them, if the fire be good, they will roast in twenty minutes;

when they are enough, lay round them bunches of asparagus, with parsley and butter for
sauce.

TO ROAST PARTRIDGES OR ANY SMALL BIRDS.

Lard them with slips of bacon, put them
on a skewer, tie it to the spit at both ends,
dredge and baste them, let them roast ten
minutes, take the crumb of half a loaf of
bread, with a piece of butter the size of a
walnut, put it in a stew pan and shake it over
a gentle fire till they are a light brown, lay
them between your birds, and pour over them
a little melted butter.

TO BOIL RABBITS.

When you have cased the rabbits, skewer
them with their heads straight up, the fore-
legs brought down, and the hind-legs straight,
boil them three quarters of an hour at least,
then smother them with onion sauce, made
the same as for boiled ducks, and serve them
up.

TO ROAST RABBITS.

When you have cased the rabbits, skewer
their heads with their mouths upon their

backs, stick their fore-legs into their ribs,
skewer the hind legs double, then make a
pudding for them of the crumb of half a loaf
of bread, a little parsley, sweet marjorum and
thyme, all shread fine, nutmeg, salt, and pepper to your taste, mix them up into a light
stuffing, with a quarter of a pound of butter,
a little good cream, and two eggs, put it into
the body and sew them up; dredge and baste
them well with lard, roast them near an hour,
serve them up with parsley and butter for
sauce, chop the livers and lay them in lumps
round the edge of the dish.

TO ROAST A CALF'S HEAD.

Wash and pick the head very nicely, having taken out the brains and tongue, prepare
a good quantity of forced meat, with veal and
suet well seasoned, fill the hole of the head
with this forced meat, skewer and tie it together upon the spit, and roast it for an hour and
a half. Beat up the brains with a little sage
and parsley shread fine, a little salt, and the
yelks of two or three eggs; boil the tongue,
peel and cut it into large dice, and fry that
and the brains, and also some of the forced

H 2

meat made up into balls, with slices of bacon. Let the sauce be strong gravy, with oysters, mushrooms, capers, and a little white wine thickened.

———

TO HASH A CALF'S HEAD.

Boil the head till the meat is almost enough for eating ; then cut it in thin slices, take three quarters of a pint of good gravy, and add half a pint of white wine, half a nutmeg, two anchovies, a small onion stuck with cloves, and a little mace ; boil these up in the liquor for a quarter of an hour, then strain it and boil it up again ; put in the meat, with salt to your taste, let it stew a little, and if you choose it, you may add some sweet breads, and make some forced meat balls with veal ; mix the brains with the yelks of eggs, and fry them to lay for a garnish. When the head is ready to be sent in, stir in a bit of butter.

———

TO BAKE A CALF'S HEAD.

Divide the calf's head, wash it clean, and having the yelks of two eggs well beaten, wash the outside of the head all over with them, and on that strew raspings of bread

sifted, pepper, salt, nutmeg, and mace powdered ; also the brains cut in pieces and
dipped in thick butter, then cover the head
with bits of butter, pour into the pan some
white wine and water, with as much gravy,
and cover it close. Let it be baked in a quick
oven, and when it is served up, pour on some
strong gravy, and garnish with slices of lemon,
red beet root pickled, fried oysters and fried
bread.

TO STUFF AND ROAST CALF'S LIVER.

Take a fresh calf's liver, and having made
a hole in it with a large knife run in length-
ways, but not quite through, have ready a
forced meat, or stuffing made of part of the
liver par-boiled, fat of bacon minced very fine,
and sweet herbs powdered ; add to these some
grated bread and spice finely powdered, with
pepper and salt. With this stuffing fill the
hole in the liver, which must be larded with fat
bacon, and then roasted, flouring it well, and
basting with butter till it is enough. This is
to be served up hot, with gravy sauce having
a little wine in it.

TO STEW WILD DUCKS.,

Having prepared the fowls, rub the insides with salt, pepper, and a little powder of cloves, put a shalot or two with a lump of butter in the body of each, then lay them in a pan that will just hold them, putting butter under and over them; cover them with vinegar and water, and add pepper, salt, whole cloves, lemon peal, and a bunch of sweet herbs; then cover the pan close and let them stew three or four hours, pass the liquor through a sieve, pour it over the ducks, and serve them up hot with a garnish of lemon sliced, and raspings of bread fried. The same way may teal, widgeons, &c. be dressed.

TO DRESS DUCKS WITH JUICE OF ORANGES.

The ducks being singed, picked, and drawn, mince the livers with a little scraped bacon, some butter, green onions, sweet herbs and parsley, seasoned with salt, pepper, and mushrooms; these being all minced together, put them into the bodies of the ducks, and roast them, covered with slices of bacon and wrapped up in paper; then put a little gravy, the juice of an orange, a few shallots minced, in a stew pan, and shake in a little pepper; when the ducks are roasted, take off the bacon, dish them, and pour your sauce with the juice of oranges over them, and serve them up hot.

TO DRESS DUCKS WITH ONIONS.

Stuff the ducks as before, cut the roots off small onions, blanch them in scalding water, then pick and put them into a stew pan with a little gravy, set them over a gentle fire, and let them simmer; when they are done, thicken them with cream and flour, and when they are roasted, dish them, and pour a ragout of onions over them, and serve them up hot.

TO MAKE A DISH OF CURRY AFTER THE EAST-INDIAN MANNER.

Cut two chickens as for fricassee, wash them clean, and put them in a stew pan with as much water as will cover them, sprinkle them with a large spoonful of salt, and let them boil till tender, covered close all the time, and skim them well; when boiled enough, take up the chickens, and put the liquor of them into a pan, then put half a pound of fresh butter in the pan, and brown it a little; put into it two cloves of garlick and a large onion sliced, and let these all fry till brown, often shaking the pan; then put in the chickens, and sprinkle over them two or three spoonsful of curry powder; then cover the pan close and let the chickens do till brown, often shaking the pan; then put in the liquor the chickens were boiled in, and let all stew till tender; if acid is agreeable, squeeze the juice of a lemon or orange in it.

DISH OF RICE, TO BE SERVED UP WITH THE CURRY IN A DISH BY ITSELF.

Take half a pound of rice, wash it clean in salt and water, then put it into two quarts of boiling water, and boil it briskly twenty minutes; then strain it in a colander and shake it into a dish, but do not touch it with your fingers nor with a spoon.

Beef, veal, mutton, rabbits, fish, &c. may be curried and sent to table with or without the dish of rice.

Curry powder is used as a fine flavoured seasoning for fish, fowl, steaks, chops, veal cutlets, hashes, minces, alamodes, turtle soup, and in all rich dishes, gravies, sauce, &c. &c.

A SEA PIE.

Lay at the bottom of a small Dutch oven some slices of boiled pork or salt beef, then potatoes and onions cut in slices, salt, pepper, thyme and parsley shread fine, some crackers soaked, and a layer of fowls cut up, or slices of veal; cover them with a paste not too rich, put another layer of each article, and cover them with paste until the oven is full; put a little butter between each layer, pour in water till it reaches the top crust, to which you must add some wine, catsup of any kind you please, and some pounded cloves; let it stew until there is just gravy enough left; serve it in a deep dish and pour the gravy on.

TO MAKE PASTE FOR THE PIE.

Pour half a pound of butter or dripping boiling hot into a quart of flour, add as much water as will make it a paste, work it and roll it well before you use it. It is quite a savoury paste.

OCRA AND TOMATAS.

Take an equal quantity of each, let the ocra be young, slice it, and skin the tomatas,

put them into a pan without water, add a
lump of butter, an onion chopped fine, some
pepper and salt, and stew them one hour.

GUMBS—A WEST INDIA DISH.

Gather young pods of ocra, wash them
clean, and put them in a pan with a little water, salt and pepper, stew them till tender, and
serve them with melted butter. They are
very nutricious and easy of digestion.

PEPPER POT.

Boil two or three pounds of tripe, cut it in
pieces, and put it on the fire with a knuckle of
veal and a sufficient quantity of water, part
of a pod of pepper, a little spice, sweet herbs
according to your taste, salt, and some dumplins ; stew it till tender, and thicken the gravy with butter and flour.

TO MAKE AN OLLA—A SPANISH DISH.

Take 2 lbs. beef, 1 lb. mutton, a chicken or
half a pullet, and a small piece of pork ; put
them into a pot with very little water, and set
it on the fire at ten o'clock to stew gently ;

you must sprinkle over it an onion chopped small, some pepper and salt, before you pour in the water ; at half after twelve, put into the pot two or three apples or pears peeled and cut in two, tomatas with the skin taken off, cimblins cut in pieces, a handful of mint chopped, lima beans, snaps, and any kind of vegetable you like, let them all stew together till three o'clock ; some cellery tops cut small and added at half after two, will improve it much.

———

ROPA VEIJA—SPANISH.

Peel the skin from ripe tomatas, put them in a pan with a spoonful of melted butter, some pepper and salt, shred cold meat or fowl, put it in and fry it sufficiently ; put slices of butter in a frying pan, add some salt and a small portion of parsley, break in six eggs, stir them quickly for a few minutes, and serve them up.

———

BEEF A-LA-DAUBE.

Get a round of beef, lard it well, and put it in a Dutch oven ; cut the meat from a shin of beef or any coarse piece in thin slices, put

J

round the sides and over the top some slices of bacon, salt, pepper, onion, thyme, parsley, cellery tops, or seed pounded, and some carrots cut small, strew the pieces of beef over, cover it with water, let it stew very gently till perfectly done, take out the round, strain the gravy, let it stand to be cold, take off the grease carefully, beat the whites of four eggs, mix a little water with them, put them to the gravy, let it boil till it looks clear, strain it, and when cold, put it over the beef.

MATELOTE OF ANY KIND OF FIRM FISH.

Cut the fish in pieces six inches long, put it in a pot with onion, parsley, thyme, mushrooms, a little spice, pepper and salt, and red wine to wet it completely, set it on a quick fire and reduce it one third, thicken with a spoonful of butter and two of flour, put it in a dish with bits of bread fried in butter, and pour the gravy over it.

CHICKEN PUDDING, A FAVORITE VIRGINIA DISH.

Beat ten eggs very light, add to them a quart of rich milk, with a quarter of a pound of butter melted, and some pepper and salt, stir in as much flour as will make a thin good batter ; take four young chickens, and after cleaning them nicely, cut off the legs, wings, &c. put them all in a sauce pan, with some salt and water and a bundle of thyme and parsley, boil them till nearly done, then take the chicken from the water and put it in the batter, pour it in a deep dish and bake it.

CHOWDER, A SEA DISH.

Take any kind of firm fish, cut it in pieces six inches long, sprinkle salt and pepper over each piece, cover the bottom of a small Dutch oven with slices of salt pork about half boiled, lay in the fish, strewing a little chopped onion between, cover with crackers that have been soaked soft in milk, pour over it two gills of wine and two of water, put on the top of the oven and stew it gently about an hour ; take it out carefully and lay it in a deep dish, thicken the gravy with a little flour and a spoonful of butter, add some chopped parsley, boil it a few minutes, and pour it over the fish ; serve it up hot.

TO MAKE POLENTA.

Put a large spoonful of butter in a quart of water, wet your corn meal with cold water in a bowl, add some salt, and make it quite smooth, then put it in the buttered water when it is hot, let it boil, stirring it continually till done ; as soon as you can handle it, make it into a ball and let it stand till quite cold, then cut it in thin slices, lay them in the bottom of a deep dish so as to cover it, put on it slices of cheese, and on that a few bits of butter, then mush, cheese, and butter, until the dish is full, put on the top thin slices of cheese, put the dish in a quick oven ; twenty or thirty minutes will bake it.

MACARONI.

Boil as much macaroni as will fill your dish, in milk and water till quite tender, drain it on a sieve, sprinkle a little salt over it, put a layer in your dish, then cheese and butter as in the polenta, and bake it in the same manner.

TO MAKE VERMICELLI.

Beat two or three fresh eggs quite light.

make them into a stiff paste with flour, knead it well and roll it out very thin, cut it in narrow strips, give them a twist, and dry them quickly on tin sheets. It is an excellent ingredient in most soups, particularly those that are thin. Noodles are made in the same manner, only instead of strips, they should be cut in tiny squares and dried. They are also good in soups.

COMMON PATTIES.

Take some veal, fat and lean, and some slices of boiled ham, chop them very fine, and season it with salt, pepper, grated nutmeg, and a small quantity of parsley and thyme minced very fine ; make some paste, cover the bottoms of small moulds, fill them with the meat, put thin lids on, and bake them crisp ; five is enough for a side dish.

EGGS IN CROQUETS.

Boil eighteen eggs, separate the yelks and whites and cut them in dice, pour over them a sauce a-la-creme, (see *eggs a-la-creme*, page 104,) add a little grated bread, mix all well together, and let it get cold ; put in some

J 2

salt and pepper, make them into cakes, cover
them well on both sides with grated bread, let
them stand an hour, and fry them a nice
brown; dry them a little before the fire, and
dish them while quite hot.

———

OMELETTE SOUFFLE.

Break six eggs, beat the yelks and whites
separately till very light, then mix them, add
four table spoonsful of powdered sugar and a
little grated lemon peel, put a quarter of a
pound of butter in a pan, when melted, pour
in the eggs and stir them; when they have
absorbed the butter, turn it on a plate previously buttered, sprinkle some powdered sugar, set it in a hot Dutch oven, and when a
little brown, serve it up for a dessert.

———

FONDUS.

Put a pint of water and a lump of butter
the size of an egg into a sauce pan, stir in as
much flour as will make a thick batter, put it
on the fire, and stir it continually till it will
not stick to the pan; put it in a bowl, and
when cold, add three quarters of a pound of
grated cheese, mix it well, then break in two

eggs, beat them well, then two more until you put in six; when it looks very light, drop it in small lumps on buttered paper, bake it in a quick oven till of a delicate brown; you may use corn meal instead of flour, for a change.

A NICE TWELVE O'CLOCK LUNCHEON.

Cut some slices of bread tolerably thick and toast them slightly, bone some anchovies, lay half of one on each toast, cover it well with grated cheese and chopped parsley mixed, pour a little melted butter on, and brown it with a salamander; it must be done on the dish you send it to table in.

TO CAVEACH FISH.

Cut the fish in pieces the thickness of your hand, wash it and dry it in a cloth, sprinkle on some pepper and salt, dredge it with flour, and fry it a nice brown; when it gets cold, put it in a pot with a little chopped onion between the layers, take as much vinegar as will cover it, mix with it some oil, pounded mace, and whole black pepper, pour it on and stop the pot closely. This is a very convenient article, as it makes an excellent and ready addition to a dinner or supper. When served up, it should be garnished with green fennel or parsley.

___

TO PICKLE STURGEON.

The best sturgeons are the small ones, about four feet long without the head, and the best part is the one next to the tail. After the sturgeon is split through the back bone, take a piece with the skin on, which is essential to its appearance and goodness, cut off the gristle, scrape the skin well, wash it, and salt it; let it lie twenty-four hours, wipe off the salt, roll it and tie it around with twine, put it on in a good deal of cold water, let it boil till you can run a straw easily into the skin, take it up, pull off the large scales, and when cold, put it in a pot, and cover it with one part vinegar and two of salt and water; keep it closely stopped, and when served, garnish with green fennel.

___

EGGS A-LA-CREME.

Boil twelve eggs just hard enough to allow you to cut them in slices, cut some crusts of bread very thin, put them in the bottom and round the sides of a moderately deep dish, place the eggs in, strewing each layer with stale bread grated and some pepper and salt.

SAUCE A-LA-CREME.

Put a quarter of a pound of butter with a large table spoonful of flour rubbed well into it, in a sauce pan, add some chopped parsley, a little onion, salt, pepper, nutmeg, and a gill of cream ; stir it over the fire until it begins to boil, then pour it over the eggs, cover the top with grated bread, set it in a Dutch oven with a heated top, and when a light brown, send it to table.

CABBAGE A-LA-CREME.

Take two good heads of cabbage, cut out the stalks, boil it tender with a little salt in the water, have ready one large spoonful of butter and a small one of flour rubbed into it, half a pint of milk, with pepper and salt, make it hot, put the cabbage in after pressing out the water, and stew it till quite tender.

TO DRESS COD FISH.

Boil the fish tender, pick it from the bones,

take an equal quantity of Irish potatoes, or parsnips boiled and chopped, and the same of onions well boiled, add a sufficiency of melted butter, some grated nutmeg, pepper, and salt, with a little brandy or wine, rub them in a mortar till well mixed ; if too stiff, liquify it with cream or thickened milk, put paste in the bottom of a dish, pour in the fish and bake it. For change, it may be baked in the form of patties.

TO MAKE CROQUETS.

Take cold fowl or fresh meat of any kind, with slices of ham, fat and lean, chop them together very fine, add half as much stale bread grated, salt, pepper, grated nutmeg, a teaspoonful of made mustard, a table spoonful of catsup, and a lump of butter ; knead all well together till it resembles sausage meat, make them in cakes, dip them in the yelk of an egg beaten, cover them thickly with grated bread, and fry them a light brown.

TO MAKE AN OMELETTE.

Break six or eight eggs in a dish, beat them a little, add parsley and chives chopped small, with pepper and salt, mix all well together.

put a piece of butter in a pan, let it melt over a clear fire till nearly brown, pour in the eggs, stir it in, and in a few minutes it will be done sufficiently; double it, and dish it quite hot.

GASPACHA—SPANISH.

Put some soft biscuit or toasted bread in the bottom of a sallad bowl, put in a layer of sliced tomatas with the skin taken off, and one of sliced cucumbers, sprinkled with pepper, salt, and chopped onion; do this until the bowl is full, stew some tomatas quite soft, strain the juice, mix in some mustard and oil, and pour over it; make it two hours before it is eaten.

EGGS AND TOMATAS.

Peel the skins from a dozen large tomatas, put four ounces butter in a frying pan, add some salt, pepper, and a little chopped onion, fry them a few minutes, add the tomatas and chop them while frying; when nearly done, break in six eggs, stir them quickly, and serve them up.

FISH SAUCE TO KEEP A YEAR.

Chop twenty-four anchovies, bones and all, ten shallots, a handful of scraped horse radish, four blades of mace, one quart of white wine, one pint of anchovy liquor, one pint of claret, twelve cloves, and twelve pepper corns; boil them together till reduced to a quart, then strain it off into a bottle for use. Two spoonsful will be sufficient for a pound of butter.

SAUCE FOR WILD FOWL.

Take a gill of claret, with as much water, some grated bread, three heads of shallots, a a little whole pepper, mace, grated nutmeg, and salt; let them stew over the fire, then beat it up with butter, and put it under the wild fowl, which being little roasted, will afford gravy to mix with this sauce.

SAUCE FOR BOILED RABBITS.

Boil the livers, and shred them very small, shred two eggs not boiled very hard, a large spoonful of grated white bread, some broth, sweet herbs, two spoonsful of white wine, one of vinegar, a little salt, and some butter; stir all together, and take care the butter does not oil.

GRAVY.

Take a rasher or two of bacon and lay it at the bottom of a stew pan, putting either veal, mutton, or beef, cut in slices, over it; then add some sliced onions, turnips, carrots, celery, a little thyme, and allspice. Put in a little water, and set it on the fire, drawing it till it be brown at the bottom, which you will know from the pan's hissing; then pour boiling water over it, and stew it an hour and a half; but the time must be regulated by the quantity. Season it with salt.

FORCEMEAT BALLS.

Take half a pound of veal, and half a pound of suet cut fine and beat in a marble mortar or wooden bowl; add a few sweet herbs shred fine, a little mace pounded fine, a small nutmeg grated, a little lemon peel, some pepper and salt, and the yelks of two eggs; mix them well together, and make them into balls and long pieces, then roll them in flour, and fry them brown. If they are for the use of white sauce, do not fry them, but put them in a sauce pan of hot water, and let them boil a few minutes.

K

SAUCE FOR BOILED DUCKS OR RABBITS.

Pour boiled onions over your ducks or rabbits prepared in this manner; peel some onions and boil them in plenty of water, then change the first water and boil them two hours. Take them up and put them in a colander to drain, and afterwards chop them on a board; then put them in a sauce pan, sprinkle a little flour over them, and put in a large piece of butter, with a little milk or cream. Set them over the fire, and when the butter is melted they will be done enough. This is a sauce for mutton.

LOBSTER SAUCE.

Boil a little mace and whole pepper long enough to take out the strong taste of the spice; then strain it off, and melt three quarters of a pound of butter in it. Cut the lobster in very small pieces, and stir it in, with anchovy, till it is tender.

SHRIMP SAUCE.

Wash half a pint of shrimps very clean, and put them in a stew pan with a spoonful of anchovy liquor, and a pound of thick melted butter; boil it up for five minutes, and squeeze in a half a lemon. Toss it up and put it in a sauce boat.

OYSTER SAUCE FOR FISH.

Scald a pint of oysters, and strain them through a sieve; then wash some more in cold water and take off their beards; put them in a stew pan and pour the liquor over them. Then add a large spoonful of anchovy liquor, half a lemon, two blades of mace, and thicken it with butter rolled in flour. Put in half a pound of butter, and boil it till it is melted; take out the mace and lemon, and squeeze the lemon juice into the sauce; boil it and stir it all the time, and put it in a boat.

CELERY SAUCE.

Wash and pare a large bunch of celery very clean, cut it into little bits, and boil it softly till it is tender. Add half a pint of cream, some mace, nutmeg, and a small piece of butter rolled in flour; then boil it gently. This is a good sauce for roasted or boiled fowls, turkeys, partridges or any other game.

MUSHROOM SAUCE.

Clean and wash one quart of fresh mushrooms, cut them in two, and put them into a
stew pan, with a little salt, a blade of mace,
and a little butter. Stew them gently for
half an hour, and then add a pint of cream
and the yelks of two eggs beat very well;
keep stirring it till it boils up, and then
squeeze in a half a lemon. Put it over the
fowls or turkies; or you may put it on a
dish, with a piece of fried bread first buttered, then toasted brown, and just dipped into
boiling water. This is a very good sauce for
white fowls of all kinds.

COMMON SAUCE.

Plain butter melted thick, with a spoonful
of walnut pickle or catsup, is a very good
sauce; but you may put as many things as
you choose into sauces.

TO MELT BUTTER.

Nothing is more simple than this process,
and nothing so generally done badly. Keep
a quart tin sauce pan with a cover to it exclusively for this purpose; weigh one quarter

of a pound of good butter, rub into it two teaspoonsful of flour ; when well mixed, put it in the sauce pan with one table spoonful of water, and a little salt ; cover it, and set the sauce pan in a larger one of boiling water, shake it constantly till completely melted and beginning to boil. If the pan containing the butter be set on coals, it will oil the butter and spoil it. This quantity is sufficient for one sauce boat. A great variety of delicious sauces can be made, by adding different herbs to melted butter, all of which are excellent to eat with fish, poultry, or boiled butchers meat. To begin with parsley—wash a large bunch very clean, pick the leaves from the stems carefully, boil them ten minutes in salt and water, drain them perfectly dry, mince them exceedingly fine, and stir them in the butter when it begins to melt. When herbs are added to butter, you must put two spoonsful of water instead of one. Chervil, young fennel, burnet, tarragon, and cress, or pepper grass, may all be used, and must be prepared in the same manner as the parsley.

——

CAPER SAUCE

Is made by mixing a sufficient quantity of

K 2

capers, and adding them to the melted butter, with a little of the liquor from the capers. Where capers cannot be obtained, pickled nasturtiums make a very good substitute, or even green pickle minced and put with the butter.

OYSTER CATSUP.

Get fine fresh oysters, wash them in their own liquor, put them in a marble mortar with salt, pounded mace, and cayenne pepper, in the proportions of one ounce salt, two drachms mace, and one of cayenne to each pint of oysters, pound them together, and add a pint of white wine to each pint ; boil it some minutes, and rub it through a sieve ; boil it again, skim it, and when cold, bottle, cork, and seal it. This composition gives a fine flavour to white sauces, and if a glass of brandy be added, it will keep good for a considerable time.

CELERY VINEGAR.

Pound two gills of celery seed, put it into a bottle, and fill it with strong vinegar ; shake it every day for a fortnight, then strain it and keep it for use. It will impart a pleasant flavour of celery to any thing with which it is used. A very delicious flavour of thyme may be obtained, by gathering it when in full perfection; it must be picked from the stalks; a large handful of it put into a jar, and a quart of vinegar or brandy poured on it, cover it very close, next day take all the thyme out, put in as much more, do this a third time, then strain it; bottle and seal it securely. This is greatly preferable to the dried thyme commonly used, during the season when it cannot be obtained in a fresh state. Mint may be prepared in the same way. The flavour of both these herbs must be preserved by care in the preparation; if permitted to stand more than twenty hours in the liquor they are infused in, a coarse and bitter taste will be extracted, particularly from mint.

TO DRESS SALAD.

To have this delicate dish in perfection, the lettuce, pepper grass, chervil, cress, &c. should be gathered early in the morning, nicely picked, washed, and laid in cold water, which will be improved by adding ice; just before din-

ner is ready to be served, drain the water
from your salad, cut it into a bowl, giving the
proper proportions of each plant ; prepare the
following mixture to pour over it : boil two
fresh eggs ten minutes, put them in water to
cool, then take the yelks in a soup plate, pour
on them a table spoonful of cold water, rub
them with a wooden spoon until they are
perfectly dissolved, then add two table spoonsful of oil ; when well mixed, put in a tea-
spoonful of salt, one of powdered sugar,
and one of made mustard ; when all these
are united and quite smooth, stir in two
table spoonsful of common, and two of tarragon vinegar ; put it over the salad, and garnish the top with the whites of the eggs cut
into rings, and lay around the edge of the
bowl young scallions, they being the most delicate of the onion tribe.

TO BOIL POTATOES.

Wash them, but do not pare or cut them
unless they are very large ; fill a sauce pan
half full of potatoes of equal size, (or make
them so by dividing the larger ones,) put to
them as much cold water as will cover them

about an inch ; they are sooner boiled, and
more savoury than when drowned in water ;
most boiled things are spoiled by having too
little water, but potatoes are often spoiled by
having too much ; they must merely be covered, and a little allowed for waste in boiling, so that they may be just covered when
done. Set them on a moderate fire till they
boil, then take them off, and set them by the
fire to simmer slowly till they are soft enough
to admit a fork ; (place no dependence on the
usual test of their skin's cracking, which, if
they are boiled fast, will happen to some potatoes when they are not half done, and the
inside is quite hard,) then pour off the water,
(if you let the potatoes remain in the water
a moment after they are done enough, they
will become waxy and watery,) uncover the
sauce pan, and set it at such a distance from
the fire as will secure it from burning ; their
superfluous moisture will evaporate, and the
potatoes will be perfectly dry and mealy.
You may afterwards place a napkin, folded
up to the size of the sauce pan's diameter,
over the potatoes, to keep them dry and mealy
till wanted. This method of managing po-

tatoes, is, in every respect, equal to steaming them; and they are dressed in half the time.

___

TO FRY SLICED POTATOES.

Peel large potatoes, slice them about a quarter of an inch thick, or cut them in shavings round and round, as you would peal a lemon; dry them well in a clean cloth, and fry them in lard or dripping. Take care that your fat and frying-pan are quite clean; put it on a quick fire, watch it, and as soon as the lard boils and is still, put in the slices of potatoes, and keep moving them till they are crisp; take them up and lay them to drain on a sieve; send them up with very little salt sprinkled on them.

___

POTATOES MASHED.

When the potatoes are thoroughly boiled, drain and dry them perfectly, pick out every speck, and rub them through a colander into a clean stew pan: to a pound of potatoes put half an ounce of butter, and a table spoonful of milk; do not make them too moist; mix them well together. When the potatoes are getting old and specked, and in

frosty weather, this is the best way of dressing them, you may put them into shapes,
touch them over with yelk of egg, and brown
them very slightly before a slow fire.

POTATOES MASHED WITH ONIONS.

Prepare some onions by putting them
through a sieve, and mix them with potatoes:
in proportioning the onions to the potatoes,
you will be guided by your wish to have more
or less of their flavour.

TO ROAST POTATOES.

Wash and dry your potatoes, (all of a size,)
and put them in a tin Dutch oven, or cheese
toaster; take care not to put them too near
the fire, or they will get burned on the outside before they are warmed through. Large
potatoes will require two hours to roast them.
To save time and trouble, some cooks half
boil them first.

TO ROAST POTATOES UNDER MEAT.

Half boil large potatoes, drain the water
from them, and put them into an earthen dish,
or small tin pan, under meat that is roasting.

and baste them with some of the dripping, when they are browned on one side, turn them and brown the other ; send them up around the meat, or in a small dish.

POTATOE BALLS.

Mix mashed potatoes with the yelk of an egg, roll them into balls, flour them, or cover them with egg and bread crumbs, fry them in clean dripping, or brown them in a Dutch oven. They are an agreeable vegetable relish, and a supper dish.

JERUSALEM ARTICHOKES

Are boiled and dressed in the various ways we have just before directed for potatoes. They should be covered with thick melted butter, or a nice white or brown sauce.

CABBAGE.

Pick cabbages very clean, and wash them thoroughly, then look them carefully over again ; quarter them if they are very large ; put them into a sauce pan with plenty of boiling water, if any skum rises, take it off, put a large spoonful of salt into the sauce pan, and boil them till the stalks feel tender. A young cabbage will take about twenty minutes, or half an hour; when full grown, nearly an hour; see that they are well covered with water all the time, and that no dirt or smoke arises from stirring the fire. With careful management, they will look as beautiful when dressed as they did when growing. Some cooks say, that it will much ameliorate the flavour of strong old cabbages to boil them in two waters, *i. e.* when they are half done, to take them out, and put them into another sauce pan of boiling water.

SAVOYS

Are boiled in the same manner; quarter them when you send them to table.

SPROUTS AND YOUNG GREENS.

The receipt written for cabbages will answer as well for sprouts, only they will be boiled enough in fifteen minutes.

ASPARAGUS.

Set a stew pan with plenty of water on the

L

fire, sprinkle a handful of salt in it, let it boil
and skim it; then put in the asparagus prepared thus: scrape all the stalks till they are
perfectly clean, throw them into a pan of cold
water as you scrape them; when they are
all done, tie them in little bundles, of a quarter of a hundred each, with bass, if you can
get it, or tape; cut off the stalks at the bottom, that they may be all of a length; when
they are tender at the stalk, which will be in
from twentyt o thirty minutes, they are done
enough. Great care must be taken to watch
the exact time of their becoming tender: take
them just at that instant, and they will have
their true flavour and colour; a minute or
two more boiling destroys both. While the
asparagus is boiling, toast a round of a loaf of
bread, about half an inch thick, brown it delicately on both sides; dip it lightly in the liquor the asparagus was boiled in, and lay it
in the middle of a dish; pour some melted
butter on the toast, and lay the asparagus upon it; let it project beyond the asparagus,
that the company may see there is a toast.
Do not pour butter over them, but send some
in a boat.

SEA KALE

Is tied up in bundles, and dressed in the same way as asparagus.

CAULIFLOWER.

Choose those that are close and white, and of a middle size, trim off the outside leaves, cut off the stalk flat at the bottom, let them lie in salt and water an hour before you boil them. Put them in boiling water with a handful of salt in it, skim it well, and let it boil slowly till done, which a small one will be in fifteen minutes, a large one in twenty, and take it up the moment it is enough; a few minutes longer boiling will spoil it.

RED BEET ROOTS

Are not so much used as they deserve to be; they are dressed in the same way as parsnips, only neither scraped nor cut till after they are boiled; they will take from an hour and a half to three hours in boiling, according to their size; to be sent to the table with salt fish, boiled beef, &c. When young, large, and juicy, it is a very good variety, an excellent garnish, and easily converted into a very cheap and pleasant pickle.

PARSNIPS

Are to be cooked just in the same manner as carrots; they require more or less time, according to their size, therefore match them in size, and you must try them by thrusting a fork into them as they are in the water; when this goes easily through, they are done enough; boil them from an hour to two hours, according to their size and freshness. Parsnips are sometimes sent up mashed in the same way as turnips, and some cooks quarter before they boil them.

CARROTS.

Let them be well washed and brushed, but not scraped; an hour is enough for young spring carrots; grown carrots must be cut in half, and will take from an hour and a half to two hours and a half. When done, rub off the peels with a clean coarse cloth, and slice them in two or four, according to their size. The best way to try if they are done enough, is to pierce them with a fork.

TURNIPS.

Peel off half an inch of the stringy outside.

full grown turnips will take about an hour and a half gentle boiling ; if you slice them, which most people do, they will be done sooner ; try them with a fork, and when tender, take them up, and lay them on a sieve till the water is thoroughly drained from them ; send them up whole ; to very young turnips, leave about two inches of green top.

___

TO MASH TURNIPS.

When they are boiled quite tender, squeeze them as dry as possible, put them into a sauce pan, mash them with a wooden spoon, and rub them through a colander ; add a little bit of butter, keep stirring them till the butter is melted and well mixed with them, and they are ready for table.

___

TURNIP TOPS

Are the shoots, which grow out, (in the spring,) from the old turnip roots. Put them into cold water an hour before they are dressed ; the more water they are boiled in the better they will look ; if boiled in a small quantity of water, they will taste bitter ; when the water boils, put in a small handful of salt, and then your vegetables; they are still better boiled with bacon in the Virginia style; if fresh and young they will be done in about twenty minutes; drain them on the back of a sieve, and put them under the bacon.

FRENCH BEANS.

Cut off the stalk end first, and then turn to the point and strip off the strings; if not quite fresh, have a bowl of spring water, with a little salt dissolved in it, standing before you, as the beans are cleansed and trimmed, throw them in; when all are done, put them on the fire in boiling water with some salt in it; when they have boiled fifteen or twenty minutes, take one out and taste it; as soon as they are tender, take them up, and throw them into a colander to drain. To send up the beans whole, when they are young, is much the best method, and their delicate flavour and colour is much better preserved. When a little more grown, they must be cut across, in two, after stringing; and for common tables, they are split, and divided across; but those who are nice, do not use them at such a growth as to require splitting.

ARTICHOKES.

Soak them in cold water, wash them well,
then put them into plenty of boiling water,
with a handful of salt, and let them boil gently till they are tender, which will take an
hour and a half, or two hours; the surest
way to know when they are done enough, is
to draw out a leaf; trim them and drain
them on a sieve, and send up melted butter
with them; which some put into small cups
so that each guest may have one.

BROCOLI.

The kind which bears flowers around the
joints of the stalks, must be cut into convenient lengths for the dish, scrape the skin
from the stalk, and pick out any leaves or
flowers that require to be removed; tie it up
in bunches, and boil it as asparagus; serve it
up hot with melted butter poured over it.
The brocoli that heads at the top like cauli-
flowers, must be dressed in the same manner
as the cauliflower.

PEAS.

To have them in perfection, they must be
quite young, gathered early in the morning,

kept in a cool place, and not shelled until they
are to be dressed ; put salt in the water, and
when it boils, put in the peas ; boil them
quick twenty or thirty minutes, according to
their age ; just before they are taken up, add
a little mint chopped very fine, drain all the
water from the peas, put in a bit of butter,
and serve them up quite hot.

PUREE OF TURNIPS.

Pare a dozen large turnips, slice them and
put them into a stew pan, with four ounces
of butter and a little salt, set the pan over a
moderate fire, turn them often with a wooden
spoon ; when they look white, add a ladle
full of veal gravy, stew them till it becomes
thick ; skim it and pass it through a sieve.

RAGOUT OF TURNIPS.

Peel as many small turnips as will fill a
dish ; put them into a stew pan with some
butter and a little sugar, set them over a hot
stove, shake them about, and turn them till
they are a good brown ; pour in half a pint of
rich high seasoned gravy, stew the turnips till
tender, and serve them with the gravy poured
over them.

RAGOUT OF FRENCH BEANS, SNAPS, STRING
BEANS.

Let them be young and fresh gathered,
string them and cut them in long thin slices,
throw them in boiling water for fifteen minutes; have ready some well seasoned brown
gravy, drain the water from the beans, put
them in the gravy, stew them a few minutes,
and serve them garnished with forcemeat
balls; there must *not* be gravy enough to
float the beans.

MAZAGAN BEANS.

This is the smallest and most delicate species of the Windsor bean. Gather them in
the morning, when they are full-grown, but
quite young, and do not shell them till you
are going to dress them. Put them into boiling water, have a small bit of middling,
(flitch,) of bacon, well boiled, take the skin
off, cover it with bread crumbs, and toast it;
lay this in the middle of the dish, drain all
the water from the beans, put a little butter
with them, and pour them round the bacon.
When the large Windsor beans are used, it
is best to put them into boiling water until

the skins will slip off, and then make
them into a puree as directed for turnips—they are very coarse when plainly
dressed.

LIMA, OR SUGAR BEANS.

Like all other spring and summer vegetables, they must be young and freshly gathered: Boil them till tender, drain them, add a
little butter, and serve them up. These
beans are easily preserved for winter use,
and will be nearly as good as fresh ones.—
Gather them on a dry day, when full grown,
but quite young: have a clean and dry keg,
sprinkle some salt in the bottom, put in a
layer of pods, containing the beans, then a
little salt, do this till the keg is full; lay a
board on, with a weight, to press them
down; cover the keg very close, and keep
it in a dry cool place—they should be put
up as late in the season, as they can be with
convenience. When used, the pods must be
washed, and laid in fresh water all night;
shell them next day, and keep them in water
till you are going to boil them ; when tender

serve them up with melted butter in a boat.
French beans (snaps) may be preserved in the
same manner.

TURNIP ROOTED CABBAGE.

The cabbage growing at the top is not good ;
cut the root in slices an inch thick, peel off
the rind, and boil the slices in a large quantity of water, till tender ; serve it up hot, with
melted butter poured over it.

EGG PLANT.

The purple ones are best, get them young
and fresh, pull out the stem, and parboil them
to take off the bitter taste ; cut them in slices
an inch thick, but do not peel them, dip them
in the yelk of an egg and cover them with
grated bread, a little salt and pepper, when
this has dried, cover the other side in the
same way ; fry them a nice brown. They
are very delicious, tasting much like soft crabs.
The egg plant may be dressed in another
manner, scrape the rind and parboil them, cut
a slit from one end to the other, take out the
seeds, fill the space with a rich forcemeat,

and stew them in well seasoned gravy, or bake them, and serve up with gravy in the dish.

POTATO PUMPKIN.

Get one of a good colour and seven or eight inches in diameter ; cut a piece off the top, take out all the seeds, wash and wipe the cavity, pare the rind off, and fill the hollow with good forcemeat, put the top on and set it in a deep pan to protect the sides ; bake it in a moderate oven, put it carefully in the dish without breaking, and it will look like a handsome mould. Another way of cooking potato pumpkin is to cut it in slices, pare off the rind, and make a puree as directed for turnips.

SWEET POTATO.

Take those that are nearly of the same size that they may be done equally, wash them clean, but do not peel them, boil them till tender, drain the water off and put them on tin sheets in a stove for a few minutes, to dry.

SWEET POTATOS STEWED.

Wash and wipe them, and if they be large cut them in two lengths; put them at the bottom of a stew-pan, lay over some slices of boiled ham, and on that, one or two chickens cut up with pepper, salt, and a bundle of herbs; pour in some water and stew them till done, then take out the herbs, serve the stew in a deep dish, thicken the gravy, and pour over it.

SWEET POTATOS BROILED.

Cut them across without peeling, in slices half an inch thick, broil them on a griddle, and serve them with butter in a boat.

SPINACH.

Great care must be used in washing and picking it clean ; drain it and throw it into boiling water—a few minutes will boil it sufficiently; press out all the water, put it in a stew-pan with a piece of butter, some pepper and salt, chop it continually with a spoon till it is quite dry; serve it with poached eggs or without as you please.

M

SORREL.

Is dressed as the spinach, and if they be mixed in equal proportions, improve each other.

CABBAGE PUDDING.

Get a fine head of cabbage, not too large, pour boiling water on, and cover it till you can turn the leaves back, which you must do carefully; take some of those in the middle of the head off, chop them fine, and mix them with rich force-meat; put this in and replace the leaves to confine the stuffing; tie it in a cloth and boil it; serve it up whole with a little melted butter in the dish.

SQUASH OR CIMLIN.

Gather young squashes, peel, and cut them in two; take out the seeds, and boil them till tender; put them into a colander, drain off the water, and rub them with a wooden spoon through the colander; then put them into a stew-pan, with a cupful of cream, a small piece of butter, some pepper and salt, stew them, stirring very frequently until dry. This is the most delicate way of preparing squashes.

WINTER SQUASH.

The crooked neck of this squash is the best part. Cut it in slices an inch thick, take off the rind and boil them with salt in the water; drain them well before they are dished, and pour melted butter over—serve them up very hot.

The large part, containing the seeds, must be sliced and pared, cut it in small pieces and stew it till soft, with just water enough to cover it, pass it through a sieve and stew it again, adding some butter, pepper, and salt; it must be dry, but not burnt. It is excellent when stewed with pork chops.

FIELD PEAS.

There are many varieties of these peas, the smaller kind are the most delicate.— Have them young and newly gathered, shell and boil them tender, pour them in a colander to drain; put some lard in a frying-pan, when it boils, mash the peas, and fry them in a cake of a light brown; put it in the dish with the crust uppermost, garnish with thin bits of fried bacon. They are very nice when fried whole, so that each pea is distinct from the other, but they must be boiled less, and fried with great care. Plain boiling is a very common way of dressing them.

CABBAGE, WITH ONIONS.

Boil them separately, and mix them in the proportions you like; add butter, pepper, and salt, and either stew them or fry them in a cake.

SALSIFY.

Scrape and wash the roots, put them into boiling water with salt; when done, drain them and place them in the dish without cutting them up. They are a very excellent vegetable, but require nicety in cooking; exposure to the air, either in scraping or after boiling, will make them black.

STEWED SALSIFY.

Half boil it, cut it up and put it in a stew-pan with a very little water and a spoonful of butter; stew them dry and serve them up. For change, you may, after stewing, cut them in scollop shells with grated bread.

and bake them; or, make them into cakes,
and fry them.—They are delicious in whatever way they can be dressed.

STEWED MUSHROOMS.

Gather grown mushrooms, but such as
are young enough to have red gills; cut off
that part of the stem which grew in the
earth, wash them carefully and take the
skin from the top; put them into a stew-
pan with some salt, but no water, stew them
till tender, and thicken them with a spoonful
of butter mixed with one of brown flour;
red wine may be added, but the flavour of
the mushroom is too delicious to require
aid from any thing.

BROILED MUSHROOMS.

Prepare them as above directed; broil
them on a griddle, and when done, sprinkle
pepper and salt on the gills, and put a little
butter on them.

TO BOIL RICE.

Put two cups full of rice in a bowl of water, rub it well with the hand, and pour off
M 2

the water ; do this until the water ceases to be discoloured, then put the rice into two and a half cups of cold water, add a teaspoonful of salt, cover the pot close, and set it on a brisk fire ; let it boil ten minutes, pour off the greater part of the water, and remove the pot to a bed of coals, where it must remain a quarter of an hour to soak and dry.

RICE JOURNEY, OR JOHNNY CAKE.

Boil a pint of rice quite soft, with a tea-spoonful of salt, mix with it while hot a large spoonful of butter, and spread it on a dish to cool ; when perfectly cold, add a pint of rice flour and half a pint of milk, beat them all to-gether till well mingled. Take the middle part of the head of a barrel, make it quite clean, wet it, and put on the mixture about an inch thick, smooth with a spoon and baste it with a little milk, set the board aslant before clear coals ; when sufficiently baked, slip a thread under the cake and turn it, baste and bake that side in a similar manner, split it and butter while hot. Small homony boiled and mixed with rice flour, is better than all rice, and if baked very thin, and afterwards toasted and buttered, it is nearly as good as cassada bread.

—

RICE MILK FOR A DESSERT.

Boil half a pint of rice in water till tender, pour off the water and add a pint of milk with two eggs beaten well stirred into it, boil all together two or three minutes, serve it up hot, and eat it with butter, sugar, and nutmeg. It may be sweetened and cooled in moulds, turned out in a deep dish, and surrounded with rich milk, with raspberry marmalade stirred into it, and strained to keep back the seeds, or the milk may be seasoned with wine and sugar.

—

OBSERVATIONS ON PUDDINGS AND CAKES.

The salt should always be washed from butter, when it is to be used in any thing that has sugar for an ingredient, and also from that which is melted to grease any kind of mould for baking, otherwise, there will be a disagreeable salt taste on the outer side of the article baked. Raisins should be stoned and cut in two, and have some flour sifted over them,

stir them gently in the flour, and take them
out free from lumps; the small quantity that
adheres to them will prevent their sticking together, or falling in a mass to the bottom.
Eggs must be fresh, or they will not beat
well; it is better to separate the yelks from the
whites always, though it is a more trouble-
some process, but for some things it is essential to do so; when they are to be mixed with
milk, let it cool after boiling, or the eggs will
poach, and only set it on the fire a few minutes to take off the raw taste of the eggs,
stirring it all the time. Currants require
washing in many waters to cleanse them;
they must be picked and well dried, or they
will stick together. Almonds should be put
in hot water till the skins will slip off, which
is called blanching; they must always be
pounded with rose or orange flower water, to
prevent their oiling. When cream is used,
put it in just before the mixture is ready;
much beating will decompose it. Before
a pudding or cake is begun, every ingredient necessary for it must be ready; when
the process is retarded by neglecting to
have them prepared, the article is injured.

'The oven must be in a proper state, and the paste in the dishes or moulds ready for such things as require it. Promptitude is necessary in all our actions, but never more-so than when engaged in making cakes and puddings. When only one or two eggs are to be used, cooks generally think it needless to beat them ; it is an error ; eggs injure every thing unless they are made light before they are used. Cloths for boiling puddings should be made of German sheeting ; an article less thick will admit the water and injure the pudding.

TO MAKE PUFF PASTE.

Sift a quart of flour, leave out a little for rolling the paste, make up the remainder with cold water into a stiff paste, knead it well, and roll it out several times ; wash the salt from a pound of butter, divide it into four parts, put one of them on the paste in little bits, fold it up, and continue to roll it till the butter is well mixed ; then put another portion of butter, roll it in the same manner ; do this till all the butter is mingled with the paste, touch it very lightly with the hands in making, bake it in a moderate oven, that will permit it to rise, but will not make it brown. Good paste must look white and as light as a feather.

———

TO MAKE MINCE MEAT FOR PIES.

Boil either calves or hogs feet till perfectly tender, rub them through a colander, when cold, pass them through again, and it will come out like pearl barley; take one quart of this, one of chopped apples, the same of currants, washed and picked, raisins, stoned and cut, of good brown sugar, suet, nicely chopped, and cider, with a pint of brandy; add a tea-spoonful of pounded mace, one of cloves and of nutmegs; mix all these together intimately. When the pies are to be made. take out as much of this mixture as may be necessary, to each quart of it add a tea-spoonful of pounded black pepper, and one of salt; this greatly improves the flavour, and can be better mixed with a small portion than with the whole mass. Cover the moulds with paste, put in a sufficiency of mince-meat, cover the top with citron, sliced thin, and lay on it a lid garnished around with paste cut in fanciful shapes. They may be eaten either hot or cold, but are best when hot.

———

TO MAKE JELLY FROM FEET.

Boil four calf's feet, that have been nicely cleaned and the hoofs taken off; when the feet are boiled to pieces, strain the liquor through a colander, and when cold, take all the grease off and put the jelly in a skillet, leaving the dregs which will be at the bottom. There should be from four feet, about two quarts of jelly ; pour into it one quart of white wine, the juice of six fresh lemons, strained from the seeds, one pound and a half of powdered loaf sugar, a little pounded cinnamon and mace, and the rind thinly pared from two of the lemons ; wash eight eggs very clean, whip up the whites to a froth, crush the shells and put with them, mix it with the jelly, set it on the fire, stir it occasionally till the jelly is melted, but do not touch it afterwards. When it has boiled till it looks quite clear on one side, and the dross accumulates on the other, take off carefully the thickest part of the dross, and pour the jelly in the bag; put back what runs through, until it comes quite transparent; then set a pitcher under the bag, and put a cover all over to keep out the dust—the jelly looks much prettier when it is broken to fill the glasses. The bag should be made of cotton or linen, and be suspended in a frame made for the purpose. The feet of hogs make the palest coloured jelly, those of sheep are a beautiful amber colour when prepared.

——

A SWEET MEAT PUDDING.

Make a quart of flour into puff paste: when done, divide it into three parts of unequal size; roll the largest out square and moderately thin, spread over it a thin layer of marmalade, leaving a margin all round about an inch broad; roll the next largest in the same manner, lay it on, cover that with marmalade, leaving a margin; then roll the smallest, and put it on the other two, spreading marmalade; fold it up, one fold over the other, the width of your hand, press the ends together, tie it in a cloth securely, and place it in a kettle of boiling water, where it can lie at length without doubling; boil it quickly, and when done, pour melted butter with sugar and wine in the dish.

TO MAKE CUSTARDS.

Boil a quart of milk with a stick of cinnamon, sweeten it to your taste; when cold, take out the cinnamon and add six eggs, well beaten; put it in cups, set them in water and make it boil till the custards are done.—Grate nutmeg on them.

SWEET-POTATO PUDDING.

Boil one pound of sweet potatos very tender, rub them while hot through a colander, add six eggs, well beaten, three quarters of a pound of powdered sugar, three quarters of butter, and some grated nutmeg and lemon-peel, with a glass of brandy; put a paste in the dish, and when the pudding is done, sprinkle the top with sugar, and cover it with bits of citron. Irish potato pudding is made in the same manner, but is not so good.

N

MACAROONE.

Blanch a pound of sweet almonds, pound them in a mortar with rose-water; whip the whites of seven eggs to a strong froth, put in one pound of powdered sugar, beat it some time, then put in the almonds, mix them well, and drop them on sheets of paper buttered; sift sugar over and bake them quickly. Be careful not to let them get discoloured.

AN ARROW ROOT PUDDING.

Boil a quart of milk, and make it into a thick batter, with arrow root; add six eggs, half a pound of butter, the same of pounded sugar, half a nutmeg, and a little grated lemon-peel; put a paste in the dish, and bake it nicely; when done, sift sugar over it, and stick slips of citron all over the top.

SAGO PUDDING.

Wash half a pound of sago in several waters; put it on to boil in a quart of milk, with a stick of cinnamon; stir it very frequently for it is apt to burn: when it becomes quite thick, take out the cinnamon, stir in half a pound of butter, and an equal quantity of sugar, with a gill of wine; when cold, add six eggs and four ounces of currants that have been plumped in hot water: bake it in a paste.

___

PUFF PUDDING.

Beat six eggs, add six spoonsful of milk, and six of flour, butter some cups, pour in the batter and bake them quickly; turn them out, and eat them with butter, sugar, and nutmeg.

___

RICE PUDDING.

Boil half a pound of rice in milk, until it is quite tender; beat it well with a wooden spoon to mash the grains; add three quarters of a pound of sugar, and the same of melted butter; half a nutmeg, six eggs, a gill of wine, and some grated lemon-peel; put a paste in the dish and bake it. For change, it may be boiled, and eaten with butter, sugar, and wine.

PLUM PUDDING.

Take a pound of the best flour, sift it,
and make it up before sunrise, with six eggs
beaten light; a large spoonful of good yeast,
and as much milk as will make it the consistence of bread; let it rise well; knead
into it half a pound of butter, put in a grated
nutmeg, with one and a half pounds of raisins stoned and cut up; mix all well together, wet the cloth, flour it, and tie it loosely, that the pudding may have room to rise.
Raisins for puddings or cakes should be rubbed in a little flour, to prevent their settling
to the bottom—see that it does not stick to
them in lumps.

ALMOND PUDDING.

Put a pound of sweet almonds in hot
water till the skin will slip off them; pound
them with a little orange flower, or rose
water, to keep them from oiling; mix with
them four crackers, finely pounded, or two
gills of rice flour; six eggs, a pint of cream,
a pound of sugar, half a pound of butter,
and four table-spoonsful of wine; put a nice
paste in the bottom of your dish, garnish

the edges, pour in the pudding, and bake in a moderate oven.

___

QUIRE OF PAPER PANCAKES.

Beat sixteen eggs, add to them a quart of milk, a nutmeg, half a pound of flour, a pound of melted butter, a pound of sugar, and two gills of wine; take care the flour be not in lumps; butter the pan for the first pancake, run them as thin as possible, and when coloured, they are done; do not turn them, but lay them carefully in the dish, sprinkling powdered sugar between each layer; serve them up hot. This quantity will make four dozen pancakes.

___

A CURD PUDDING.

Put two quarts of milk on the fire; when it boils, pour in half a pint of white wine; strain the curd from the whey, and pound it in a mortar, with six ounces of butter, and half a pound of loaf sugar, and half a pint of rice flour, or as much crackers, beaten as fine as flour; six eggs made light, and half a grated nutmeg; beat all well together and bake them in saucers in a moderate

N 2

oven; turn them out carefully in your dish, stick thin slices of citron in them, and pour on rich melted butter, with sugar and wine.

LEMON PUDDING.

Grate the rind from six fresh lemons, squeeze the juice from three, and strain in it; beat the yelks of sixteen eggs very light; put to them sixteen table-spoonsful of powdered loaf sugar, not heaped up; add the grated rind and the juice, with four crackers finely pounded; beat it till light, put a puff paste in your dish, pour the pudding in, and bake it in a moderate oven; it must not be very brown.

BREAD PUDDING.

Grate the crumb of a stale loaf, and pour on it a pint of boiling milk, let it stand an hour, then beat it to a pulp; add six eggs, well beaten, half a pound of butter, the same of powdered sugar, half a nutmeg, a glass of brandy, and some grated lemon-peel; put a paste in the dish and bake it.

THE HENRIETTA PUDDING.

Beat six eggs very light; sift into them a pound of loaf sugar powdered, and a light pound of flour, with half a grated nutmeg and a glass of brandy; beat all together very well; add a pint of cream, pour it in a deep dish and bake it: when done, sift some powdered sugar over it.

TANSEY PUDDING.

Beat seven eggs very light, mix with them a pint of cream, and nearly as much spinach juice, with a little juice of tansey; add a quarter of a pound of powdered crackers or pounded rice made fine, a glass of wine, some grated nutmeg, and sugar; stir it over the fire to thicken, pour it into a paste and bake it.

CHERRY PUDDING.

Beat six eggs very light, add half a pint of milk, 6 oz. flour, 8 oz. grated bread, 12 oz. suet, chopped fine, a little salt: when it is beat well, mix in 18 oz. preserved cherries or damsins; bake or boil it. Make a sauce of melted butter, sugar, and wine.

APPLE PIE.

Put a crust in the bottom of a dish, put on it a layer of ripe apples pared and sliced thin, then a layer of powdered sugar; do this alternately till the dish is full; put in a few tea-spoonsful of rose-water and some cloves; put on a crust and bake it.

BAKED APPLE PUDDING.

Take well-flavoured apples, bake, but don't burn them; rub them through a sieve, take one pound of the apples, so prepared, mix with it, while hot, half a pound of butter, and half a pound of powdered sugar; the rinds of two lemons, grated, and when cold, add six eggs, well beaten; put a paste in the bottom of a dish, and pour in the apples; half an hour will bake it; sift a little sugar on the apples when baked.

A NICE BOILED PUDDING.

Make up a pint of flour at sun-rise, exactly as you do for bread; see that it rises well; have a large pot of water boiling, and half an hour before the puddings are to go to table, make the dough in balls, the size of a goose-egg; throw them in the water and boil them quickly, keeping the pot covered. they must be torn asunder, as cutting will make them heavy; eat them with powdered sugar, butter, and grated nutmeg.

___

AN EXCELLENT AND CHEAP PUDDING.

Wash a pint of small homony very clean, and boil it tender, add an equal quantity of corn meal, make it into a batter with eggs, milk, and a piece of butter; bake it like batter cakes on a griddle, and eat it with butter and molasses.

___

SLICED APPLE PUDDING.

Beat six eggs very light, add a pint of rich milk, pare some apples, or peaches, slice them thin, make the eggs and milk into a tolerably thick batter with flour, add a small cup of melted butter, put in the fruit, and bake it in a deep dish; eat with sugar, butter, and nutmeg.

___

BAKED INDIAN MEAL PUDDING.

Boil one quart of milk, mix in it two gills and a half of corn meal very smoothly, seven eggs well beaten, a gill of molasses, and a good piece of butter; bake it two hours.

BOILED INDIAN MEAL PUDDING.

Mix one quart of corn meal with three quarts of milk, take care it be not lumpy, add three eggs and a gill of molasses; it must be put on at sunrise, to eat at three o'clock; the great art in this pudding is tying the bag properly, as the meal swells very much.

PUMPKIN PUDDING.

Stew a fine sweet pumpkin till soft and dry, rub it through a sieve, mix with the pulp six eggs quite light, a quarter of a pound of butter, half a pint of new milk, some pounded ginger and nutmeg, a wine glass of brandy, and sugar to your taste. Should it be too liquid, stew it a little dryer; put a paste round the edges and in the bottom of a shallow dish or plate, pour in the mixture, cut some thin bits of paste, twist them and lay them across the top and bake it nicely.

COMPOTE OF APPLES.

Pare and core the apples, and if you pre-

fer it, cut them in four, wash them clean, and
put them in a pan with water and sugar
enough to cover them ; add cinnamon, and lemon peal which has been previously soaked,
scraped on the inside, and cut in strings ;
boil them gently until the apples are done,
take them out in a deep dish, boil the syrup to
a proper consistency, and pour it on them.

CHARLOTTE.

Stew any kind of fruit, and season it in any
way you like best ; fry some slices of bread
in butter, put them, while hot, in the bottom
and round the sides of a dish which has been
rubbed with butter, put in your fruit, and lay
slices of bread on the top ; bake it a few minutes, turn it carefully into another dish,
sprinkle on some powdered sugar, and glaze
it with a salamander.

APPLE FRITTERS.

Pare some apples and cut them in thin
slices, put them in a bowl, with a glass of
brandy, some white wine, a quarter of a
pound of pounded sugar, a little cinnamon
finely powdered and the rind of a lemon

grated ; let them stand some time, turning them over frequently ; beat two eggs very light, add one quarter of a pound of flour, a tablespoonful of melted butter, and as much cold water as will make a thin batter ; drip the apples on a sieve, mix them with the batter, take one slice with a spoonful of butter to each fritter, fry them quick, of a light brown, drain them well, put them in a dish, sprinkling sugar over each, and glaze them nicely.

BELL FRITTERS.

Put a piece of butter the size of an egg into a pint of water, let it boil a few minutes, thicken it very smoothly with a pint of flour, let it remain a short time on the fire, stir it all the time that it may not stick to the pan, pour it in a wooden bowl, add five or six eggs, breaking one and beating it in, then another, and so on till they are all in and the dough quite light, put a pint of lard in a pan, let it boil, make the fritters small, and fry them of a fine amber colour.

BREAD FRITTERS.

Cut your bread of a convenient size, pour

on it some white wine, and let it stand a few
minutes, drain it on a sieve, beat four eggs
very light, add four spoonsful of wine, beat
all well together, have your lard boiling, dip
the bread in the egg, and fry it a light brown;
sprinkle sugar on each and glaze them.

TO MAKE MUSH.

Put a lump of butter the size of an egg into a quart of water, make it sufficiently thick
with corn meal and a little salt; it must be
mixed perfectly smooth, stir it constantly till
done enough.

TO MAKE JUMBALS.

To one pound of butter and one of flour,
add one pound of sugar, four eggs beaten
light, and whatever spice you like; knead
all well together, and bake it nicely.

TO MAKE DROP BISCUIT.

Beat eight eggs very light, add to them
twelve ounces of flour, and one pound of sugar; when perfectly light, drop them on tin
sheets, and bake them in a quick oven.

O

TAVERN BISCUIT.

To one pound of flour, add half a pound of sugar, half a pound of butter, some mace and nutmeg powdered, and a glass of brandy or wine ; wet it with milk, and when well kneaded, roll it thin, cut it in shapes, and bake it quickly.

FLUMMERY.

One measure of jelly, one of cream, and half a one of wine ; boil it fifteen minutes over a slow fire, stirring all the time, sweeten it, and add a spoonful of orange flour or rose water ; cool it in a mould, turn it in a dish, and pour around it cream seasoned in any way you like.

RUSK.

Rub half a pound of sugar into three pounds of flour, sift it, pour on half a pint of good yeast, beat six eggs, add half a pint of milk, mix all together, and knead it well ; if not soft enough, add more milk ; it should be softer than bread ; make it at night ; in the morning, if well risen, work in six ounces of butter, and bake it in small rolls; when cold, slice it, lay it on tin sheets, and dry it in the oven.

———

GINGER BREAD.

Three quarts of flour, three quarters of a pound of brown sugar, a large spoonful of pounded ginger, one teaspoonful of powdered cloves, sift it, melt half a pound of butter in a quart of rich molasses, wet the flour with it, knead it well, and bake it in a slack oven.

———

PLEBEIAN GINGER BREAD.

Mix three large spoonsful of pounded ginger with three quarts of flour, sift it, dissolve three teaspoonsful of pearl ash in a cup of water, and pour it on the flour; melt half a pound of butter in a quart of molasses, mix it with the flour, knead it well, cut it in shapes, and bake it.

———

SUGAR GINGER BREAD.

Take two pounds of the nicest brown sugar, dry and pound it, put it into three quarts of flour, add a large cup full of powdered ginger and sift the mixture; wash the salt out of a pound of butter, and cream it ; have twelve eggs well beaten, work into the butter first the mixture, then the froth from the eggs, until all are in and it is quite light, add a glass of brandy ; butter shallow moulds, pour it in, and bake in a quick oven.

DOUGH NUTS—A YANKEE CAKE.

Dry half a pound of good brown sugar, pound it and mix it with two pounds of flour and sift it ; add two spoonsful of yeast, and as much new milk as will make it like bread; when well risen, knead in half a pound of butter, make in cakes the size of a half dollar, and fry them a light brown in boiling lard.

RAISEN CAKE.

Take three pounds of flour, one and a half of pounded sugar, a teaspoonful of cloves, one of mace and one of ginger all finely powdered, pass the whole through a sieve ; put to it four spoonsful of good yeast and twelve eggs, mix it up well, and if not sufficiently soft, add a little milk ; make it up at night, and set it to rise; when well risen, knead into it a pound

of butter and two gills of brandy ; have ready two pounds of raisins stoned, mix all well
together, pour it into a mould of proper size,
and bake it in an oven heated as for bread ;
let it stand till thoroughly done, and do not
take it from the mould until quite cold.

___

POUND CAKE.

Wash the salt from a pound of butter and
rub it till it is soft as cream, have ready a
pound of flour sifted, one of powdered sugar,
and twelve eggs well beaten ; put alternately
into the butter, sugar, flour, and the froth
from the eggs ; continuing to beat them together till all the ingredients are in, and the
cake quite light ; add some grated lemon
peel, a nutmeg, and a gill of brandy ; butter
the pans and bake them. This cake makes
an excellent pudding if baked in a large
mould, and eaten with sugar and wine. It is
also excellent when boiled, and served up with
melted butter, sugar, and wine.

___

SAVOY, OR SPUNGE-CAKE.

Take twelve fresh eggs, put them in the
scale and balance them with sugar ; take

out half and balance the other half with flour; separate the whites from the yelks, whip them up very light, then mix them and sift in, first sugar, then flour, till both are exhausted; add some grated lemon-peel, bake them in paper cases or little tin moulds. This, also, makes an excellent pudding, with butter, sugar, and wine for sauce.

A RICH FRUIT CAKE.

Have the following articles prepared before you begin the cake; four pounds of flour dried and sifted; four pounds of butter washed to free it from salt; two pounds of loaf sugar pounded, a quarter of a pound of mace, the same of nutmegs powdered; wash four pounds of currants clean, pick and dry them, blanch one pound of sweet almonds, and cut them in very thin slices, stone two pounds of raisins, cut them in two, and strew a little flour over, to prevent their sticking together, and two pounds of citron sliced thin; break thirty eggs, separating the yelks and whites; work the butter to a cream with your hand, put in, alternately.

flour, sugar, and the froth from both whites
and yelks, which must be beaten separately,
and *only* the froth put in. When all are mixed, and the cake looks very light, add the
spice, with half a pint of brandy, the currants and almonds; butter the mould well,
pour in part of the cake, strew over it some
raisins and citron, do this until all is in: set
it in a well heated oven, when it has risen,
and the top is coloured, cover it with paper;
it will require three hour's baking—it must
be iced.

NAPLES BISCUIT.

Beat twelve eggs light, add to them one
pound of flour, and one of powdered sugar;
continue to beat all together till perfectly
light; bake it in long pans, four inches wide,
with divisions, so that each cake, when done,
will be four inches long, and one and a half
wide.

SHREWSBURY CAKES.

Cream one pound of butter, add a pound
of powdered sugar, with a pound and a half
of flour, six eggs, a grated nutmeg, and a

gill of brandy; work it well, roll it thin, and cut it in shapes; put them on tin sheets, and bake without discolouring them.

LITTLE PLUM CAKES.

Prepare them as directed for pound cake, add raisins and currants, bake them in small tin shapes, and ice them.

NICE BUNS.

Put four ounces of sugar with three quarters of a pound of flour, make it up with two spoonsful of yeast, and half a pint of milk; when well risen, work into it four ounces of butter, make it into small buns, and bake them in a quick oven; do not burn them.

AN ENGLISH PLUM PUDDING.

Beat eight eggs very light, add to them a pound of flour sifted, and a pound of powdered sugar; when it looks quite light, put in a pound of suet finely shread, a pint of milk, a nutmeg grated and a gill of brandy; mix with it a pound of currants, washed, picked, and dried, and a pound of raisins stoned and floured, tie it in a thick cloth, and boil it steadily eight hours.

MARROW PUDDING.

Grate a large loaf of bread, and pour on the crumbs a pint of rich milk boiling hot; when cold, add four eggs, a pound of beef marrow sliced thin, a gill of brandy with sugar and nutmeg to your taste; mix all well together, and either bake or boil it; when done, stick slices of citron over the top.

SIPPET PUDDING.

Cut a loaf of bread as thin as possible, put a layer of it in the bottom of a deep dish, strew on some slices of marrow or butter, with a handful of currants or stoned raisins, do this till the dish is full; let the currants or raisins be at the top; beat four eggs, mix with them a quart of milk that has been boiled a little and become cold, a quarter of a pound of sugar, and a grated nutmeg; pour it in and bake it in a moderate oven; eat it with wine sauce.

BURNT CUSTARD.

Boil a quart of milk, and when cold, mix with it the yelks of eight eggs; stir them together over the fire a few minutes, sweeten it to your taste, put some slices of savoy cake in the bottom of a deep dish, and pour on the custard ; whip the whites of the eggs to a strong froth, lay it lightly on the top, sift some sugar over it, and hold a salamander over it until it is a light brown; garnish the top with raspberry marmalade, or any kind of preserved fruit.

EDINBURG SWEET CREAM.

Take skimmed milk that has only acquired a moderately acid taste, put it in an upright wooden vessel with a machine for drawing it off, place it in a tub, and pour hot water in the tub till it rises nearly as high as the milk in the vessel; cover the whole with a cloth to keep in the heat. In a few hours the milk separates into two parts; the upper part assuming the consistency of thick cream, that has very much the appearance of good cream, only moderately acid ; the other portion that remains is a thin watery liquid, which is of a pungent acid taste, and may be easily drawn off. The cream is then fit for use. Much of the goodness of this depends upon the skill of the maker, as it is greatly affected by various circumstances, particularly by the degree of heat to which it is subjected, and the acidity of the milk. It is eaten with sugar and nutmeg, and considered a great delicacy.

TO MAKE BREAD.

When you find the barrel of flour a good one, empty it into a chest or box made for the purpose, with a lid that will shut close; it keeps much better in this manner than when packed in a barrel, and even improves by lying lightly; sift the quantity you intend to make up, put into a bowl three quarters of a pint of cold water to each quart of flour, with a large spoonful of yeast, and a little salt, to every quart; stir into it just as much of the flour as will make a thin batter, put half the remaining flour in the bottom of a tin kettle, pour the batter on it, and cover it with the other half; stop it close, and set it where it can have a moderate degree of warmth. When it has risen well, turn it into a bowl, work in the dry flour and knead it some minutes, return it into the kettle, stop it, and give it moderate heat. In the morning, work it a little, make it into rolls, and bake it. In the winter, make the bread up at three o'clock, and it will be ready to work before bed time. In summer, make it up at five o'clock. A quart of flour should weigh just one pound and a quarter.

PATENT YEAST.

Put half a pound of fresh hops into a gallon of water and boil it away to two quarts, then strain it and make it a thin batter with flour ; add half a pint of good yeast, and when well fermented, pour it in a bowl and work in as much corn meal as will make it the consistency of biscuit dough ; set it to rise, and when quite light, make it into little cakes, which must be dried in the shade, turning them very frequently ; keep them securely from damp and dust. Persons who live in towns, and can procure brewer's yeast, will save trouble by using it ; take one quart of it, add a quart of water, and proceed as before directed.

TO PREPARE THE CAKES.

Take one or more cakes, according to the flour you are to make; pour on a little warm water ; when it is dissolved, stir it well, thicken with a little flour, and set it near the fire to rise before it is used. The best thing to keep yeast in, is a small mug or pitcher, with a close stopper, under which must be placed a double fold of linen to make it still closer. This is far preferable to a bottle, and more easily cleaned.

TO MAKE NICE BISCUIT.

Rub a large spoonful of butter into a quart of risen dough, knead it well and make it into biscuit, either thick or thin ; bake them quickly.

MUFFINS.

Sift a quart of flour, put to it a little salt, and a large spoonful of yeast ; beat the white of a fresh egg to a strong froth, add it, and make the flour up with cold water as soft as you can to allow it to be handled ; set it in a moderately warm place. Next morning, beat it well with a spoon, put it on the griddle in a round form, and bake nicely, turning them frequently till done.

P

FRENCH ROLLS.

Sift a quart of flour, add a little salt, a spoonful of yeast, two eggs well beaten, and half a pint of milk, knead it and set it to rise ; next morning, work in an ounce of butter, make the dough into small rolls, and bake them. The top crust should not be hard.

CRUMPETS.

Take a quart of dough from your bread at a very early hour in the morning, break three fresh eggs, separating the yelks from the whites, whip them both to a froth, mix them with the dough, and add gradually milk warm water, till you make a batter the thickness of buck wheat cakes ; beat it well, and set it to rise till near breakfast time ; have the griddle ready, pour on the batter to look quite round ; they do not require turning.

APOQUINIMINC CAKES.

Put a little salt, one egg beaten, and four ounces of butter, in a quart of flour ; make it into a paste with new milk, beat it for half an hour with a pestle, roll the paste thin, and cut it into round cakes ; bake them on a grid-iron and be careful not to burn them.

BATTER CAKES.

Boil two cups of small hominy very soft, add an equal quantity of corn meal with a little salt, and a large spoonful of butter ; make it in a thin batter with three eggs, and a sufficient quantity of milk, beat all together some time, and bake them on a griddle or in waffle irons. When eggs cannot be procured, yeast makes a good substitute ; put a spoonful in the batter, and let it stand an hour to rise.

BATTER BREAD.

Take six spoonsful of flour and three of corn meal, with a little salt ; sift them and make a thin batter with flour, eggs, and a sufficient quantity of rich milk ; bake it in little tin moulds in a quick oven.

CREAM CAKES.

Melt as much butter in a pint of milk as will make it rich as cream, make the flour into a paste with this, knead it well, roll it out frequently, cut it in squares, and bake on a griddle.

SOUFFLE BISCUITS.

Rub four ounces of butter into a quart of

flour, make it into paste with milk, knead it well, roll it as thin as paper, and bake it to looke white.

====

CORN MEAL BREAD.

Rub a piece of butter the size of an egg into a pint of corn meal, make a batter with two eggs and some new milk, add a spoonful of yeast, set it by the fire an hour to rise, butter little pans and bake it.

====

SWEET POTATO BUNS.

Boil and mash a potato, rub into it as much flour as will make it like bread, add spice and sugar to your taste, with a spoonful of yeast; when it has risen well, work in a piece of butter; bake it in small rolls, to be eaten hot with butter, either for breakfast or tea.

====

RICE WAFFLES.

Boil two cups of rice quite soft, make it into a thick batter with two eggs, a spoonful of butter, and some milk; beat it till light, and bake it in waffle irons.

====

VELVET CAKES.

Make a batter of one quart of flour, three

eggs, a quart of milk and a gill of yeast; when well risen, stir in a large spoonful of melted butter, and bake them in muffin hoops.

CHOCOLATE CAKES.

Put half a pound of nice brown sugar into a quart of flour, sift it and make it into a paste with four ounces of butter melted in as much milk as will wet it; knead it till light, roll it tolerably thin, cut it in strips an inch wide, and just long enough to lay in a plate; bake then on a griddle, put them in the plate in rows to checker each other and serve them to eat with chocolate.

WAFERS.

Make a very thin batter with eggs, milk, butter, and powdered loaf sugar, to your taste; pour it into wafer-irons, bake them very quick, without browning; roll them as you take them from the irons.

BUCK-WHEAT CAKES.

Put a large spoonful of yeast and a little salt into a quart of buck-wheat meal, make it into a batter with cold water; let it rise well and bake it on a griddle; it turns sour very quickly if it be allowed to stand any time after it has risen.

ICE CREAMS.

When ice creams are not put into shapes, they should always be served in glasses with handles.

VANILLA CREAM.

Boil a Vanilla bean in a quart of rich milk until it has imparted the flavour sufficiently; then take it out, and mix with the milk, eight eggs, yelks and whites, beaten well; let it boil a little longer—make it very sweet, for much of the sugar is lost in the operation of freezing.

RASPBERRY CREAM.

Make a quart of rich boiled custard; when cold, pour it on a quart of ripe red raspberries, mash them in it, pass it through a sieve, sweeten and freeze it.

STRAWBERRY CREAM

Is made in the same manner; the strawber-

ries must be very ripe and the stems picked
out. If rich cream can be procured, it will
be infinitely better—the custard is intended
as a substitute when cream cannot be had.

COCOA-NUT CREAM.

Take the nut from its shell, pare it, and
grate it very fine; mix it with a quart of
cream, sweeten and freeze it. If the nut
be a small one, it will require one and a
half to flavour a quart of cream.

CHOCOLATE CREAM.

Scrape a quarter of a pound of chocolate
very fine, put it in a quart of milk, boil it till
the chocolate is dissolved, stirring it continually ; thicken with six eggs. A vanilla bean
boiled with the milk, will improve the flavour greatly.

OYSTER CREAM.

Make a rich soup, (see directions for oyster soup,) strain it from the oysters, and
freeze it.

ICED JELLY.

Make calf's foot jelly, not very stiff, freeze
it and serve it in glasses.

PEACH CREAM.

Get fine soft peaches, perfectly ripe, peel them, take out the stones, and put them in a China bowl; sprinkle some sugar on and chop them very small, with a silver spoon; if the peaches be sufficiently ripe, they will become a smooth pulp; add as much cream or rich milk as you have peaches; put more sugar and freeze it.

COFFEE CREAM.

Toast two gills of raw coffee till it is a light brown, and not a grain burnt; put it hot from the toaster, without grinding it, into a quart of rich, and perfectly sweet, milk; boil it, and add the yelks of eight eggs: when done, strain it through a sieve, and sweeten it—if properly done, it will not be discoloured. The coffee may be dried, and will answer for making in the usual way to drink, allowing more for the quantity of water, than if it had not gone through this process.

QUINCE CREAM.

Wash ripe quinces, and boil them whole,

till quite tender, let them stand to drain and cool; then rub them through a hair sieve; mix with the pulp as much cochineal, finely powdered, as will make it a pretty colour; then add an equal quantity of cream, and sweeten it. Pears or apples may be used, prepared in the same manner.

CITRON CREAM.

Cut the finest citron melons, when perfectly ripe, take out the seeds and slice the nicest part into a China bowl, in small pieces, that will lie conveniently, cover them with powdered sugar, and let them stand several hours, then drain off the syrup they have made, and add as much cream as it will give a strong flavour to, and freeze it. Pine apples may be used in the same way.

ALMOND CREAM.

Pour hot water on the almonds, and let them stand till the skins will slip off, then pound them fine, and mix them with cream; a pound of almonds, in the shells, will be sufficient for a quart of cream; sweeten and freeze it. The kernels of the common black walnut, prepared in the same way, make an excellent cream.

LEMON CREAM.

Pare the yellow rind very thin from four lemons, put them in a quart of fresh cream, and boil it; squeeze and strain the juice of one lemon, saturate it complete with powdered sugar, and when the cream is quite cold, stir it in; take care that it does not curdle—if not sufficiently sweet, add more sugar.

LEMONADE ICED.

Make a quart of rich lemonade, whip the whites of six fresh eggs to a strong froth; mix them well with the lemonade, and freeze it. The juice of morello cherries, or of currants mixed with water and sugar, and prepared in the same way, make very delicate ices.

OBSERVATIONS ON ICE CREAM.

It is the practice with some indolent cooks, to set the freezer, containing the cream, in a tub with ice and salt, and put it in the ice-house; it will certainly freeze there, but

not until the watery particles have subsided,
and by the separation destroyed the cream.
A freezer should be twelve or fourteen inches deep, and eight or ten wide. This faci-
litates the operation very much, by giving a
larger surface for the ice to form, which it
always does on the sides of the vessel; a
silver spoon, with a long handle, should be
provided for scraping the ice from the sides,
as soon as formed, and when then the whole
is congealed, pack it in moulds (which must
be placed with care, lest they should not be
upright,) in ice and salt till sufficiently hard
to retain the shape—they should not be turned out till the moment they are to be served.
The freezing tub must be wide enough to
leave a margin of four or five inches all
around the freezer when placed in the middle, which must be filled up with small
lumps of ice mixed with salt—a larger tub
would waste the ice. The freezer must be
kept constantly in motion during the process,
and ought to be made of pewter, which is
less liable than tin to be worn in holes, and
spoil the cream by admitting the salt water.

TO MAKE CUSTARD.

Make a quart of milk quite hot that it may not whey when baked; let it stand to get cold, and then mix six eggs with it; sweeten it with loaf sugar, and fill the custard cups, put on the covers, and set them in a Dutch oven with water, but not enough to risk its boiling into the cups; do not put on the top of the oven. When the water has boiled ten or fifteen minutes, take out a cup, and if the custard be the consistence of jelly, it is sufficiently done, serve them in the cups, with the covers on, and a tea-spoon on the dish between each cup;— grate nutmeg on the tops when cold.

TO MAKE A TRIFLE.

Put slices of Savoy cake or Naples biscuit at the bottom of a deep dish, wet it with white wine, and fill the dish nearly to the top with rich boiled custard; season half a pint of cream with white wine and sugar, whip it to a froth; as it rises, take it lightly off and lay it on the custard; pile it up high and tastely; decorate it with preserves of of any kind, cut so thin as not to bear the froth down by its weight.

FLOATING ISLAND.

Have the bowl nearly full of syllabub, made with white wine and sugar ; beat the whites of six new laid eggs to a strong froth, then mix with it raspberry or strawberry marmalade enough to flavour and colour it ; lay the froth lightly on the syllabub, first putting in some slices of cake, raise it in little mounds, and garnish with something light.

SYLLABUB.

Season the milk with sugar and white wine, but not enough to curdle it ; fill the glasses nearly full, and crown them with whipt cream seasoned.

LEMON CREAM.

Pare the rind very thin from four fresh lemons, squeeze the juice and strain it, put them both into a quart of water, sweeten it to your taste, add the whites of six eggs beat to a froth, set it over the fire, and keep stirring until it thickens, but don't let it boil, then pour

Q

it in a bowl; when cold, strain it through a sieve, put it on the fire, and add the yelks of the eggs; stir it till quite thick and serve it in glasses.

ORANGE CREAM

Is made in the same manner, but requires more juice to give a flavour.

RASPBERRY CREAM.

Stir as much raspberry marmalade into a quart of cream as will be sufficient to give a rich flavour of the fruit, strain it and fill your glasses, leaving out a part to whip into froth for the top.

TEA CREAM.

Put one ounce of the best tea in a pitcher, pour on it a table-spoon of water, and let it stand an hour to soften the leaves; then put to it a quart of boiling cream, cover it close, and in half an hour strain it; add four teaspoonsful of a strong infusion of rennet in water, stir it and set it on some hot ashes and cover it; when you find, by cooking a little of it, that it will jelly, pour it into glasses, and garnish with thin bits of preserved fruit.

SAGO CREAM.

Wash the sago clean, and put it on the fire with a stick of cinnamon and as much water as will boil it thick and soft; take out the cinnamon and add rich boiled custard till it is of a proper thickness, sweeten it, and serve in glasses or cups with grated nutmeg on the top.

BARLEY CREAM

Is made the same way ; you may add a little white wine to both, it will give an agreeable flavour.

GOOSEBERRY FOOL.

Pick the stems and blossoms from two quarts of green gooseberries, put them in a stew pan with their weight in loaf sugar and a very little water ; when sufficiently stewed, pass the pulp through a sieve, and when cold, add rich boiled custard till it is like thick cream ; put it in a glass bowl and lay the frothed cream on the top.

TO MAKE SLIP.

Fill a deep dish with rich milk made warm,

set it on hot ashes, and add rennet enough to set it; when it becomes jellied, put the dish on ice to cool, pour cream on the top, and eat it with powdered sugar and nutmeg. It is a most delicious dish for dessert in summer, but must not be made too long before it is served, or it will lose its delicacy and become tough; neither must there be too much rennet. The proper quantity can only be ascertained by practice, as some rennet bags are stronger than others.

CURDS AND CREAM.

Put as much rennet into rich milk as will set it; when the curd is formed, take it up carefully with an egg spoon to drain off the whey, lay it in a deep dish, and surround it with cream; eat it with powdered sugar. This arcadian dish must be made with judgement, lest the curd be hard.

BLANC MANGE.

Break one ounce of isinglass into very small pieces, wash it well, and pour on a pint of boiling water; next morning add a quart of milk, boil it till the isinglass is dissolved, strain it, put in two ounces sweet almonds, blanched and pounded; sweeten it and put it in the mould; when stiff, turn them into a deep dish, and put raspberry cream around them. For a change, stick thin slips of blanched almonds all over the blanc mange, and dress round with syllabub nicely frothed. Some moulds require colouring; for an ear of corn, mix the yelk of an egg, with a little of the blanc mange, fill the grains of the corn with it, and when quite set, pour in the white, but take care it is not warm enough to melt the yellow: for a bunch of asparagus, colour a little with spinach juice, to fill the green tops of the heads. Fruit must be made the natural colour of what it represents. Cochineal and alkanet root, pounded and dissolved in brandy, make good colouring, but blanc mange should never be served without raspberry cream, or syllabub to eat with it.

TO MAKE A HEN'S NEST.

Get five small eggs, make a hole at one end and empty the shells, fill them with blanc mange, when stiff and cold, take off

Q 2

the shells; pare the yellow rind very thin from six lemons, boil them in water till tender, then cut them in thin strips to resemble straw, and preserve them with sugar; fill a small deep dish half full of nice jelly, when it is set put the straw on, in form of a nest, and lay the eggs in it. It is a beautiful dish for a dessert or supper.

FISH IN JELLY.

Fill a deep glass dish half full of jelly—have as many small fish-moulds as will lie conveniently in it, fill them with blanc mange; when they are cold, and the jelly set, lay them on it as if going in different directions; put in a little more jelly, and let it get cold to keep the fish in their places, then fill the dish so as to cover them. The jelly should be made of hog's feet, very light-coloured and perfectly transparent.

Little dishes for a second course or supper:

PHEASANTS, A-LA-DAUB.

Roast two pheasants in the nicest manner: get a deep dish, the size and form of the one you intend to serve the pheasants in—it must be as deep as a tureen; put in savoury jelly about an inch and a half at the bottom; when that is set and the pheasants cold, lay them on the jelly, with their breasts down; fill the dish with jelly up to their backs, take care it is not warm enough to melt the other, and that the birds are not displaced; just before it is to be served, set it a moment in hot water to loosen it; put the dish on the top, and turn it out carefully.

PARTRIDGES A-LA-DAUB.

Truss six partridges neatly, cover them with thin slices of fat bacon, taken from the top of a middling, this keeps them white, and gives a good flavour; they must be wrapped entirely in it; roast them, and when done, take off the bacon; let them get cold, and use jelly as for the pheasants.

FISH A-LA-DAUB.

Boil as many large white perch as will be sufficient for the dish; do not take off their heads, and be careful not to break their skins; when cold, place them in the dish, and cover

them with savoury jelly broken. A nice
piece of rock-fish is excellent done in the
same way.

CHICKENS A-LA-DAUB.

Roast two half-grown chickens, cut off
the legs and wings, pull the breast from each
side entire, take the skin from all the pieces,
lay it in the dish, and cover it with jelly.

TO MAKE SAVOURY JELLY.

Put eight or ten pounds of coarse lean
beef, or the same quantity of the inferior
parts of the fore quarter of veal, into a pot
with two gallons of water; a pound of lean
salt pork, three large onions chopped, three
carrots, a large handful of parsley, and any
sweet herb that you chose, with pepper and
salt; boil it very gently till reduced to two
quarts; strain it through a sieve; next day
take off the fat, turn out the jelly, and separate it from the dregs at the bottom; put it
on the fire with half a pint of white wine,
a large spoonful of lemon pickle, and the
whites and shells of four eggs beaten: when
it boils clear on one side, run it through the
jelly bag.

TURKEY A-LA-DAUB.

Bone a small turkey, put pepper and salt on the inside, and cover it with slices of boiled ham or tongue; fill it with well-seasoned forcemeat, sew it up and boil it:—cover it with jelly.

SALMAGUNDI.

Turn a bowl on the dish, and put on it, in regular rings, beginning at the bottom, the following ingredients, all minced: anchovies with the bones taken out, the white meat of fowls, without the skin, hard boiled eggs, the yelks and whites chopped separately, parsley, the lean of old ham scraped, the inner stalks of celery; put a row of capers round the bottom of the bowl, and dispose the others in a fanciful manner; put a little pyramid of butter on the top, and have a small glass with egg mixed as for sallad to eat with the salmagundi.

AN EXCELLENT RELISH AFTER DINNER.

Put some soup or gravy from any of the dishes on the table, into the stew-dish; add a good portion of pepper, vinegar, wine, catsup, and salt; let it be very highly seasoned; broil the legs, liver, and gizzard, of a turkey, the kidney of veal, or any thing you fancy: cut it up in small pieces when broiled, put it in the gravy and stew it at table.

TO STEW PERCH.

Lay the perch in a deep dish with the heads on; sprinkle salt, pepper, and a little chopped onion over each layer; when they are all in, take as much water as will be sufficient to fill the dish a little more than half full; add a gill of wine, one of catsup, a little lemon pickle, and spice; cover the dish with a tin sheet, set it in the oven, and let it stew gently till done; when it is cold, take out the fish, without breaking, and put them in another dish, with the jelly attached to them.

DIRECTIONS FOR MAKING PRESERVES.

The preserving pan should be made of bell metal, flat at the bottom, very large in diameter but not deep. It should have a cover to fit closely, and handles at the sides of the pan, for taking it off with ease when the syrup boils too fast. There should also be a large chafingdish with long legs, for the convenience of moving it to any part of the room. The process is a tedious one, and if the superintendant be not comfortably situated, the preserves cannot be properly managed. A ladle the size of a saucer, pierced, and having a long handle, will be necessary, for taking up the fruit without syrup. When a chafingdish cannot be procured, the best substitute is a brick stove with a grating to burn charcoal The sugar should be the best double refined, but if the pure amber coloured sugar house syrup from the West Indies can be got, it is greatly superior ; it never ferments, and the trouble is very much lessened by having ready made syrup, in which it is only necessary to boil the fruit till clear. All delicate fruit should be done gently and not allowed to remain more than half an hour after it begins to stew, before it is laid on dishes to cool ; it must be put into the syrup again for the same time ; continue this until it is sufficiently transparent. The advantage of this method is, that the preserves are less liable to boil to pieces, than when done all at one time. It is injudicious to put more in the pan at once than can lie on the bottom without crowding. The pan must be made bright, and nothing permitted to cool in it, lest it should canker. Delicate preserves should be kept in small glasses or pots that will not hold more than one or two pounds, for the admission of air injures them ; put letter paper wet with brandy on the preserves, and cover the tops with many folds of soft paper that will tie round closely ; keep them in a dry place, and expose them occasionally to the sun to check fermentation ; fruit for preserving should be in full perfection, but not too ripe.

TO PRESERVE CLINGSTONE PEACHES.

Get the finest yellow clingstones, pare them and lay them in a bowl, have their weight of sugar pounded, and sprinkle it over them as they are put in ; let them stand two or three hours, put them together with the sugar into the pan, add a little water, and let the peaches remain till thoroughly scalded, take them out with the ladle, draining off the syrup ; should there not be enough to cover the peaches, add more water, boil it and skim it.

return the fruit, and do them gently till quite clear. Have some stones cracked, blanch the kernels, and preserve them with the peaches.

CLINGSTONES SLICED.

Pare the peaches and cut them in as large slices as possible, have their weight in sugar, and preserve them as the others.

SOFT PEACHES.

Get yellow soft peaches that are not quite ripe, pare and divide them, scrape the places where the stones lay with a teaspoon, and follow the former directions.

PEACH MARMALADE.

Take the ripest soft peaches, (the yellow ones make the prettiest marmalade,) pare them and take out the stones ; put them in the pan with one pound of dry light coloured brown sugar to two of peaches ; when they are juicy they do not require water ; with a silver or wooden spoon, chop them with the sugar, continue to do this, and let them boil gently till they are a transparent pulp that will be a jelly when cold. Puffs made of this marmalade are very delicious.

R

PEACH CHIPS.

Slice them thin, and boil them till clear in a syrup made with half their weight of sugar, lay them on dishes in the sun, and turn them till dry ; pack them in pots with powdered sugar sifted over each layer ; should there be syrup left, continue the process with other peaches. They are very nice when done with pure honey instead of sugar.

PEARS.

The small pears are better for preserving than large one. Pare them and make a syrup with their weight of sugar and a little water, leave the stem on, and stick a clove in the blossom end of each ; stew them till perfectly transparent.

PEAR MARMALADE.

Boil the pears till soft ; when cold, rub the pulp through a sieve and boil it to a jelly, allowing one pound of sugar to two of pears.

QUINCES.

Select the finest and most perfect quinces, lay them on shelves, but do not let them touch each other, keep them till they look yellow and have a fragrant smell; put as many in the preserving pan as can lie conveniently, cover them with water and scald them well, then take out the cores and put them in water, cover the pan and boil them some time, strain the water, add to it the weight of the quinces in pounded loaf sugar, dissolve and skim it, pare the quinces, put them in the pan, and should there not be syrup enough to cover them, add more water; stew them till quite transparent. They will be light coloured if kept covered during the process, and red if the cover be taken off. Fill the space the cores occupied with quince jelly before they are put into the pots, and cover them with syrup.

QUINCE JELLY.

Prepare the quinces as before directed, take off the stems and blossoms, wash them clean, and cut them in slices without paring; fill the pan and pour in water to cover them, stew them gently, putting in a little water occasionally, till they are soft; then pour them into a jelly bag, let all the liquor run through without pressing it, which must be set aside for the best jelly ; to each pint of this put a pound of loaf sugar pounded, and boil it to a jelly. The bag may be squeezed for an inferior, but a very nice jelly.

QUINCE MARMALADE.

Boil the quinces in water until soft, let them cool, and rub all the pulp through a sieve ; put two pounds of it to one of sugar, pound a little cochineal, sift it through fine muslin, and mix it with the quince to give a colour ; pick out the seeds, tie them in a muslin bag, and boil them with the marmalade ; when it is a thick jelly, take out the seeds and put it in pots.

CHERRIES.

The most beautiful cherries to preserve are the carnation, and common light red, with short stems ; select the finest that are not too ripe ; take an equal weight with the cherries of double refined sugar, make it into a syrup, and preserve them without stoning and with the stems on : if they be done carefully, and the " Directions for preserv ing" closely attended to, the stems wil l not come off, and they will be so transparen t. that the stones may be seen.

———

MORELLO CHERRIES.

Take out the stones with a quill over a deep dish, to save the juice that runs from them ; put to the juice, a pound of sugar for each pound of cherries, weighed after they are stoned ; boil and skim the syrup, then put in the fruit and stew till quite clear.

———

TO DRY CHERRIES.

Stone them and save the juice ; weigh the cherries and allow one pound of good brown sugar to three of the fruit ; boil it with the juice, put the cherries in, stew them fifteen or twenty minutes, take them out, drain off the syrup, and lay the cherries in dishes to dry in the sun ; keep the syrup to pour over, a little at a time, as it dries on the cherries, which must be frequently turned over ; when all the syrup is used, put the cherries away in pots, sprinkling a little powdered loaf sugar between the layers. They make excellent pies, puddings, and charlottes.

R 2

RASPBERRY JAM.

To each pound of ripe red, or English raspberries, put one pound of loaf sugar; stir it frequently, and stew till it is a thick jelly.

TO PRESERVE STRAWBERRIES.

Get the largest strawberries before they are too ripe; have the best loaf sugar, one pound to each of strawberries; stew them very gently, taking them out to cool frequently, that they may not be mashed;—when they look clear, they are done enough.

STRAWBERRY JAM

Is made in the same manner as the raspberry, and is very fine to mix with cream, for blanc mange, puffs, sweet-meat puddings, &c. &c.

GOOSEBERRIES.

Select young gooseberries, make a syrup with one pound of loaf sugar, to each of fruit; stew them till quite clear, and the syrup becomes thick, but do not let them be mashed. They are excellent made into tarts; do not cover the pan while they are stewing.

APRICOTS IN BRANDY.

Take freshly gathered apricots, not too ripe; to half their weight of loaf sugar, add as much water as will cover the fruit, boil and skim it; then put in the apricots, and let them remain five or six minutes; take them up without syrup, and lay them on dishes to cool; boil the syrup till reduced one half: when the apricots are cold, put them in bottles and cover them with equal quantities of syrup and French brandy. If the apricots be cling-stones, they will require more scalding.

PEACHES IN BRANDY.

Get yellow soft peaches, perfectly free from defect, and newly gathered, but not too ripe; place them in a pot and cover them with cold weak lie, turn over those that float frequently, that the lie may act equally on them; at the end of an hour, take them out, wipe them carefully with a soft cloth, to get off the down and skin, and lay

them in cold water; make a syrup as for
the apricots, and proceed in the same manner,
only scald the peaches more.

CHERRIES IN BRANDY.

Get the short stemmed bright red cherries, in bunches; make a syrup with equal
quantities of sugar and cherries, scald the
cherries, but do not let the skins crack,
which they will do if the fruit be too ripe.

MAGNUM BONUM PLUMS IN BRANDY.

Select those that are free from blemish,
make a syrup with half their weight of sugar, and preserve them in the same manner
directed for apricots—green gages. The
large amber, and the blue plums, are also
excellent done in the same way.

LEMON PICKLE.

Grate the yellow rind from two dozen fine
fresh lemons, quarter them, but leave them
whole at the bottom, sprinkle salt on them,
and put them in the sun every day until dry;
then brush off the salt, put them in a pot with
one ounce of nutmegs and one of mace

pounded, a large handful of horse radish scraped and dried, two dozen cloves of garlic, and a pint of mustard seed; pour on one gallon of strong vinegar, tie the pot close, put a board on, and let it stand three months; strain it, and when perfectly clear bottle it.

TOMATA CATSUP.

Gather a peck of tomatas, pick out the stems, and wash them; put them on the fire without water, sprinkle on a few spoonsful of salt, let them boil steadily an hour, stirring them frequently, strain them through a colander, and then through a sieve; put the liquid on the fire with half a pint of chopped onions, a quarter of an ounce of mace broke into small pieces, and if not sufficiently salt, add a little more, one tablespoonful of whole black pepper, boil all together until just enough to fill two bottles; cork it tight.—Make it in August.

TOMATA MARMALADE.

Gather full grown tomatas while quite green, take out the stems and stew them till soft, rub them through a sieve; put the pulp on the fire seasoned highly with pepper, salt, and pounded cloves; add some garlic, and stew all together till thick; it keeps well, and is excellent for seasoning gravies, &c. &c.

TOMATA SWEET MARMALADE.

Prepare it in the same manner, mix some loaf sugar with the pulp, and stew until it is a stiff jelly.

PEPPER VINEGAR.

Get one dozen pods of pepper when ripe, take out the stems, and cut them in two; put them in a kettle with three pints of vinegar, boil it away to one quart and strain it through a sieve. A little of this is excellent in gravy of every kind, and gives a flavour greatly superior to black pepper; it is also very fine when added to each of the various catsups for fish sauce.

MUSHROOM CATSUP.

Take the flaps of the proper mushrooms from the stems, wash them, add some salt, and crush them; then boil them some time, strain them through a cloth, put them on the fire again with salt to your taste, a few cloves of garlic, and a quarter of an ounce of cloves pounded, to a peck of mushrooms; boil it till reduced to less than half the original quantity, bottle and cork it well.

TARRAGON, OR ASTRAGON VINEGAR.

Pick the tarragon nicely from the stem, let it lie in a dry place forty-eight hours, put it in a pitcher, and to one quart of the leaves put three pints of strong vinegar; cover it close, and let it stand a week; then strain it, and after standing in the pitcher till quite clear, bottle it and cork it closely.

CURRY POWDER.

One ounce turmerick, one do. coriander seed, one do. cummin seed, one do. white ginger, one of nutmeg, one of mace, and one of cayenne pepper; pound all together, and pass them through a fine sieve; bottle and cork it well; one teaspoonful is sufficient to season any made dish.

TO PICKLE CUCUMBERS.

Gather them full grown, but quite young; take off the green rind, and slice them tolerably thick; put a layer in a deep dish, strew over it some chopped onion and salt, do this until they are all in; sprinkle salt on the top, let them stand six hours, put them in a colander, when all the liquor has run off, put them in a pot, strew a little cayenne pepper over each layer, and cover them with strong cold vinegar; when the pot is full, pour on some sweet oil and tie it up close.

OIL MANGOS.

Gather the melons a size larger than a goose egg, put them in a pot, pour boiling salt and water made strong upon them, and cover them up; next day, cut a slit from the stem to the blossom end, and take out the seeds carefully, return them to the brine, and let them remain in it eight days; then put them in strong vinegar for a fortnight, wipe the insides with a soft cloth, stuff them and tie them, pack them in a pot with the slit uppermost, strew some of the stuffing over each layer, and keep them covered with the best vinegar.

TO MAKE THE STUFFING FOR FORTY MELLONS.

Wash a pound of white race ginger very clean, pour boiling water on it, and let it stand twenty-four hours; slice it thin, and dry it; one pound of horse radish scraped and dried, one pound of mustard seed washed and dried, one pound of chopped onion, one ounce mace, one of nutmeg pounded fine, two ounces of turmeric, and a handful of whole black pepper; make these ingredients into a paste with a quarter of a pound of mus'ard and a large cup full of sweet oil; put a clove of garlic into each mango.

TO PREPARE VINEGAR FOR GREEN OR YELLOW PICKLE.

One pound of ginger sliced and dried, one of horse radish scraped and dried, one of mustard seed washed and dried, one ounce long pepper, an ounce of mace and one of nutmegs finely pounded; put all these ingredients in a pot, pour two gallons of strong vinegar on, and let it stand twelve months, stirring it very frequently. When this vinegar is used for the pickles, put two gallons more vinegar, with some mace and nutmegs, and keep it for another year. The articles for the yellow pickle must be scalded, dried, and soaked a fortnight in plain vinegar with some turme-

S

ric in it; then put them in a pot, and pour
on the prepared vinegar, mixing some turmeric with it. The green pickles should be
made green by pouring boiling salt and water
on them every morning for several days, and
covering them close to keep in the steam; as
they become green, put them in vinegar and
turmeric, and at the end of the fortnight, put
them in a pot, and cover them with the prepared vinegar, adding some turmeric. When
the prepared vinegar is poured from the ingredients, do it very carefully, that it may be
quite clear. Pickles keep much better when
the vinegar is not boiled. The turmeric
should be mixed up with oil, and made thin
with vinegar before it is put into the pickle pot.
Should the green pickles at any time loose
their colour, it may be restored by adding a
little more turmerick. All pickles are best
when one or two years old.

TO PICKLE ONIONS.

Get white onions that are not too large,
cut the stem close to the root with a sharp
knife, put them in a pot, pour on boiling salt
and water to cover them, stop the pot close-

ly, let them stand a fortnight, changing the salt and water every three days; they must be stirred daily, or those that float will become soft; at the end of this time, take off the skin and outer shell, put them in plain cold vinegar with a little turmeric. If the vinegar be not very pale, the onion will not be of a good colour.

TO PICKLE NASTERTIUMS.

Gather the berries when full grown, but young, put them in a pot, pour boiling salt and water on, and let them stand three or four days; then drain off the water, and cover them with cold vinegar; add a few blades of mace and whole grains of black pepper.

TO PICKLE RADISH PODS.

Cut them in nice bunches as soon as they are fully formed; they must be young and tender: pour boiling salt and water on them, cover with a thick cloth and pewter plate, to keep in the steam; repeat this every day till they are a good green, then put them in cold vinegar, with mace and whole pepper;

mix a little turmeric with a small portion of oil, and stir it into the vinegar; it will make the pods of a more lively green. They are very pretty for garnishing meats.

TO PICKLE ENGLISH WALNUTS.

The walnuts should be gathered when the nut is so young that you can run a pin into it easily; pour boiling salt and water on and let them be covered with it nine days, changing it every third day; take them out and put them on dishes in the air for a few minutes, taking care to turn them over; this will make them black much sooner; put them in a pot, strew over some whole pepper, cloves, a little garlic, mustard seed, and horse radish scraped and dried, cover them with strong cold vinegar.

TO PICKLE PEPPER.

Gather the large bell pepper when quite young, leave the seeds in and the stem on, cut a slit in one side, between the large veins, to let the water in; pour boiling salt and water on, changing it every day or three weeks—you must keep them closely stopped;

if, at the end of this time, they be a good green, put them in pots and cover them with cold vinegar and a little turmeric; those that are not sufficiently green, must be continued under the same process till they are so. Be careful not to cut through the large veins, as the heat will instantly diffuse itself through the pod.

___

TO MAKE WALNUT CATSUP.

Gather the walnuts as for pickling, and keep them in salt and water the same time; then pound them in a marble mortar; to every dozen walnuts, put a quart of vinegar; stir them well every day for a week, then put them in a bag and press all the liquor through; to each quart, put a tea-spoonful of pounded cloves, and one of mace, with six cloves of garlic; boil it fifteen or twenty minutes and bottle it.

___

TO PICKLE GREEN NECTARINES OR APRICOTS.

Gather them while the shell is soft; green them with salt and water, as before directed;

when a good green, soak them in plain vinegar for a fortnight, and put them in the yellow pickle-pot.

———

TO PICKLE ASPARAGUS.

Pour boiling salt and water on, and cover them close; next day take them out, dry them, and after standing in vinegar, put them with the yellow pickle. The intention of keeping all pickles in plain vinegar, previous to their being put in the prepared pot, is to draw off the water with which they are saturated, that they may not weaken the vinegar of the pot. The best way to dry all articles for yellow pickle, is to take advantage of a clear hot day, and put them in full sun-shine, on a table covered with a soft thick cloth, pinning the corners round the table, to prevent its blowing up over the articles; the cloth absorbs the moisture, and by turning them frequently on a dry place, they become white, and of course take the colour of the turmeric better: one day of clear hot sun-shine is sufficient to prepare them for the first vinegar.

GINGER WINE.

To three gallons of water, put three pounds of sugar and four ounces of race ginger, washed in many waters to cleanse it; boil them together for one hour, and strain it through a sieve; when luke-warm, put it in a cask, with three lemons cut in slices, and two gills of beer yeast; shake it well and stop the cask very tight; let it stand a week to ferment, and if not clear enough to bottle, it must remain until it becomes so; it will be fit to drink in ten days after bottling.

ORGEAT,
A necessary Refreshment at all Parties.

Boil two quarts of milk with a stick of cinnamon, and let it stand to be quite cold, first taking out the cinnamon; blanch four ounces of the best sweet almonds, pound them in a marble mortar with a little rose-water; mix them well with the milk, sweeten it to your taste, and let it boil a few minutes only, lest the almonds should be oily; strain it through a very fine sieve, till quite smooth and free from the almonds; serve it up either cold or luke-warm in glasses with handles.

CHERRY SHRUB.

Gather ripe morello cherries, pick them from the stalk, and put them in an earthen pot, which must be set into an iron pot of water; make the water boil, but take care that none of it gets into the cherries; when the juice is extracted, pour it into a bag made of tolerably thick cloth which will permit the juice to pass, but not the pulp of your cherries; sweeten it to your taste, and when it becomes perfectly clear, bottle; put a gill of brandy into each bottle before you pour in the juice, cover the corks with rosin. It will keep all summer in a dry cool place, and is delicious mixed with water.

CURRANT WINE.

Gather full ripe currants on a dry day, pick them from the stalks, and weigh them; then crush them with your hands, leaving none whole; for every two pounds of currants put one quart of water, stir all well together, and let it stand three hours, and strain the liquor through a sieve; then, for every three pounds of currants, put one pound of powdered loaf sugar, stir it till the sugar is dissolved, boil it,

and keep skimming it as long as any scum
will rise ; let it stand sixteen hours to cool before you put it in the cask ; stop it very close.
If the quantity be twenty gallons, let it stand
three weeks before you bottle it ; if it be
thirty gallons, it must remain a month ; it
should be perfectly clear when drawn off ;
put a lump of sugar in each bottle, cork it
well, and keep it in a cool place, or it will
turn sour. This is a pleasant and cheap wine,
and if properly made, will keep good for
many years. It makes an agreeable beverage
for the sick, when mixed with water.

TO MAKE CHERRY BRANDY.

Get equal quantities of morello and common black cherries, fill your cask, and pour
on (to a ten gallon cask) one gallon of boiling water ; in two or three hours, fill it up
with brandy, let it stand a week, then draw
off all, and put another gallon of boiling water, and fill it again with brandy ; at the end
of the week, draw the whole off, empty the
cask of the cherries, and pour in your brandy
with water to reduce the strength ; first dis-
solving one pound of brown sugar in each

gallon of your mixture. If the brandy be very strong, it will bear water enough to make the cask full.

ROSE BRANDY.

Gather leaves from fragrant roses without bruising, fill a pitcher with them, and cover them with French brandy ; next day, pour off the brandy, take out the leaves, and fill the pitcher with fresh ones, and return the brandy ; do this till it is strongly impregnated, then bottle it ; keep the pitcher closely covered during the process. It is better than distilled rose water for cakes, &c.

PEACH CORDIAL.

Gather ripe clingstone peaches, wipe off the down, cut them to the stone in several places, and put them in a cask ; when filled with peaches, pour on as much peach brandy as the cask will hold, let it stand six or eight weeks, then draw it off, put in water until reduced to the strength of wine ; to each gallon of this, add one pound of good brown sugar, dissolve it, and pour the cordial into a cask just large enough to hold it ; when perfectly clear it is fit for use.

RASPBERRY CORDIAL.

To each quart of ripe red raspberries, put one quart of best French brandy, let it remain about a week, then strain it through a sieve or bag, pressing out all the liquid ; when you have got as much as you want, reduce the strength to your taste with water, and put a pound of powdered loaf sugar to each gallon; let it stand till refined. Strawberry cordial is made the same way. It destroys the flavour of these fruits to put them on the fire.

RASPBERRY VINEGAR.

Put a quart of ripe red raspberries in a bowl ; pour on them a quart of strong well-flavoured vinegar, let them stand 24 hours, strain them through a bag, put this liquid on another quart of fresh raspberries, which strain in the same manner, and then on a third quart ; when this last is prepared, make it very sweet with pounded loaf sugar ; re-fine and bottle it. It is a delicious beverage mixed with iced water.

MINT CORDIAL.

Pick the mint early in the morning, while

the dew is on it, and be careful not to bruise it ; pour some water over it and drain it ; put two handsful into a pitcher with a quart of French brandy, cover it and let it stand till next day; take the mint carefully out, and put in as much more, which must be taken out next day ; do this the third time ; then put three quarts of water to the brandy, and one pound of loaf sugar powdered ; mix it well together, and when perfectly clear, bottle it.

HYDROMEL, OR MEAD.

Mix your mead in the proportion of 36 oz. of honey to four quarts of warm water ; when the honey is completely held in solution, pour it into a cask. When fermented, and become perfectly clear, bottle and cork it well. If properly prepared, it is a pleasant and wholesome drink, and in summer, particularly, grateful on account of the large quantity of carbonic acid gas, which it contains. Its goodness, however, depends greatly on the *time* of bottling, and other circumstances, which can only be acquired by practice.

LEMON CORDIAL.

Cut six fresh lemons in thin slices, put them into a quart and a half of milk, boil it until the whey is very clear, then pass it through a sieve; put to this whey, one and a half quarts of French brandy, and three pounds of powdered loaf sugar; stir it till the sugar is dissolved; let it stand to refine, and bottle it: pare some of the yellow rind of the lemons very thin, and put a little in each bottle.

———

SPRUCE BEER.

Boil a handful of hops, and twice as much of the chippings of sassafras root, in ten gallons of water; strain it, and pour in, while hot, one gallon of molasses, two spoonsful of the essence of spruce, two spoonsful of powdered ginger, and one of pounded allspice; put it in a cask: when sufficiently cold, add half a pint of good yeast; stir it well, stop it close, and when ferment-ed and clear, bottle it, and cork it tight.

———

MOLASSES BEER.

Put five quarts of hops, and five of wheat

T

bran, into fifteen gallons of water; boil it three or four hours, strain it, and pour it into a cask with one head taken out; put in five quarts of molasses, stir it till well mixed, throw a cloth over the barrel; when moderately warm, add a quart of good yeast, which must be stirred in; then stop it close with a cloth and board. When it has fermented and become quite clear, bottle it :— the corks should be soaked in boiling water an hour or two, and the bottles perfectly clean and well drained.

———

TO KEEP LEMON-JUICE.

Get lemons quite free from blemish, squeeze them and strain the juice; to each pint of it, put a pound of good loaf sugar pounded; stir it frequently until the sugar is completely dissolved, cover the pitcher closely, and let it stand till the dregs have subsided, and the syrup is transparent; have bottles perfectly clean and dry, put a wine-glass full of French brandy into each bottle, fill it with syrup, cork it and dip the neck into melted rosin or pitch; keep them in a cool dry cellar—do not put it on the fire, it will destroy the fine flavour of the juice.

Pour water on the peels of the lemons, let them soak till you can scrape all the white pulp off, then boil the peel till soft; preserve them with half their weight of sugar, and keep them for mince-pies, cakes, &c.: they are a very good substitute for citron.

SUGAR VINEGAR.

To one measure of sugar, put seven measures of water, moderately warm; dissolve it completely; put it into a cask, stir in yeast, in the proportion of a pint to eight gallons : stop it close, and keep it in a warm place till sufficiently sour.

HONEY VINEGAR.

To one quart of clear honey, put eight quarts of warm water; mix it well together: when it has passed through the acetous fermentation, a white vinegar will be formed, in many respects better than the ordinary vinegar.

SYRUP OF VINEGAR.

Boil two pounds of sugar with four quarts

of vinegar, down to a syrup, and bottle it. This makes an excellent beverage when mixed with water, either with or without the addition of brandy. It is nearly equal in flavour to the syrup of lime juice, when made with superior vinegar.

AROMATIC VINEGAR.

Put a portion of acetate of potash, (sal diureticus,) into a smelling bottle, mix gradually with it half its weight of sulphuric acid, and add a few drops of oil of lavender.

VINEGAR OF THE FOUR THIEVES.

Take lavender, rosemary, sage, wormwood, rue, and mint, of each a large handful; put them in a pot of earthen ware, pour on them four quarts of very strong vinegar, cover the pot closely, and put a board on the top; keep it in the hottest sun two weeks, then strain and bottle it, putting in each bottle a clove of garlic. When it has settled in the bottle and become clear, pour it off gently; do this until you get it all free from sediment. The proper time to make it is when the herbs are in full vigour, in June. This vinegar is very refreshing in crowded rooms, in the apartments of the sick, and is peculiarly grateful when sprinkled about the house in damp weather.

LAVENDER WATER.

Put a pint of highly rectified spirits of wine, to one ounce of essential oil of lavender, and two drachms of ambergris; shake them well together and keep it closely stopped.

HUNGARIAN WATER.

One pint spirits of wine, one ounce oil of rosemary, and two drachms essence of ambergris.

TO PREPARE COSMETIC SOAP FOR WASHING THE HANDS.

Take a pound of castile or any other nice old soap, scrape it in small pieces, and put it on the fire with a little water; stir it till it becomes a smooth paste, pour it into a bowl, and when cold, add some lavender water, or essence of any kind, beat it with a silver spoon until well mixed, thicken it with corn meal, and keep it in small pots closely covered, for the admission of air will soon make the soap hard. T 2

SOFT POMATUM.

Get nice sweet lard that has no salt in it, put in any agreeable perfume, beat it to a cream, and put it in small pots.

TO MAKE SOAP.

Put on the fire any quantity of lie you chuse that is strong enough to bear an egg, to each gallon add three quarters of a pound of clean grease, boil it very fast and stir it frequently; a few hours will suffice to make it good soap. When you find by cooling a little on a plate that it is a thick jelly and no grease appears, put in salt in the proportion of one pint to three gallons, let it boil a few minutes and pour it in tubs to cool; (should the soap be thin, add a little water to that in the plate, stir it well, and by that means ascertain how much water is necessary for the whole quantity; very strong lie will require water to thicken it after the incorporation is complete; this must be done before the salt is added.) Next day, cut out the soap, melt it, and cool it again; this takes out all the lie, and keeps the soap from shrinking when dried. A strict conformity to these rules will banish

the lunar bugbear which has so long annoyed
soap makers. Should cracknels be used,
there must be one pound to each gallon. Kitchen grease should be clarified in a quantity
of water, or the salt will prevent its incorpo-
rating with the lie. Soft soap is made in the
same manner only omitting the salt. It may
also be made by putting the lie and grease
together in exact proportions, and placing it
under the influence of a hot sun for eight or ten
days, stirring it well four or five times a day.

—

TO MAKE STARCH.

Wash a peck of good wheat and pick it very clean, put it in a tub and cover it with water; it must be kept in the sun, and the water
changed every day, or it will smell very offen-
sively. When the wheat becomes quite soft,
it must be well rubbed in the hands, and the
husks thrown into another tub; let this white
substance settle, then pour off the water, put
on fresh, stir it up well, and let it subside; do
this every day till the water comes off clear;
then pour it off, collect the starch in a bag,
tie it up tight, and set it in the sun a few days,
then open it and dry the starch on dishes.

TO CLEAN SILVER UTENSILS.

Dissolve a piece of allum in strong lie, skim it carefully, mix in it some soap, wash the silver, and dry it with a clean cloth.

TO MAKE BLACKING.

A quarter of a pound of ivory black, two ounces of sugar candy, a quarter of an ounce of gum tragacanth, pound them all very fine, boil a bottle of porter, and stir the ingredients in while boiling hot.

TO CLEAN KNIVES AND FORKS.

Wash them in warm water and wipe them till quite dry, then touch them lightly over without smearing the handles, with rotten stone made wet ; let it dry on them, and then rub with a clean cloth until they are bright. With this mode of cleaning, one set of knives and forks will serve a family twenty years ; they will require the frequent use of a steel to keep them with a keen edge, but must never be put into very hot water, lest the handles be injured.

TO MAKE CANDLES.

Have the moulds quite clean, and put very nice wick into them ; cut the tallow in small pieces, put it into a tin vessel with a spout to it, set it in boiling water, and stir it until the tallow is melted, then fill the moulds ; do not let it boil, for that makes it oily and it will scale off. When the candles are cold, wipe the moulds with a cloth dipped in hot water until they can be drawn with ease.

APPENDIX I
Bibliographical Notes
by Karen Hess on
The Virginia House-wife.

So that the reader may have all of Mrs. Randolph's recipes in one volume, I here present thirty-five recipes that first appeared in *The Virginia House-wife . . . Second edition, with amendments and additions. Washington: 1825,* and six that first appeared in *The Virginia House-wife, or Methodical Cook. By Mrs. Mary Randolph . . . Third edition . . . Washington: 1828.* (In previous editions, the preface was signed *M. Randolph* but her name was not on the title page. *House-wife* lost its hyphen beginning with the fourth edition, 1830.) I also include, in facsimile, an interesting plan for a home refrigerator, along with her explanatory notes, as found uniquely in the 1825 edition. Three recipes that appeared in the first edition were thereafter excised; a fourth was severely cut. This annotated facsimile edition thus represents, I believe, the only complete text of *The Virginia House-wife*.

The additional recipes had to be transcribed because they had been interspersed throughout the work. I transcribed them as they first appeared. (All parentheses are original; my notations are marked by brackets.) I note this because minor details of spelling and punctuation were changed in succeeding editions.

It is the 1831 edition, copyright 1828 (the two editions being virtually identical), that went down in succeeding editions. (The date on the preface, otherwise unchanged from 1824, was fudged to 1831 in spite of her death three years earlier.) By 1860, the book had gone through nineteen editions, according to Lowenstein. (I hear of editions as late as 1888 but have not verified them.) By that time, the devastating effects of the iron range were making *The Virginia House-wife* seem rather old-fashioned; housewives wanted recipes for the new-fangled puffy cakes. But many of Mrs. Randolph's recipes lived on; no work has been more ruthlessly pillaged than this classic, so much so that it is pointless to single out examples (a number were even translated into Pennsylvania German at mid-century in *Die Geschickte Hausfrau* [1852], as pointed out by William Woys Weaver in his forthcoming translation of the work under the title of *Sauerkraut Yankees*.)

Mrs. Randolph prided herself on her methodical approach to cookery. Would that she had applied it to the organization and indexing of her book: johnny cakes were inserted following vegetables, *Forcemeat Balls* among the sauces, ice creams following cakes, and *Salmagundi* and *a-la-daub* recipes among the *Cold Creams*. Inept editorial attempts to tidy things up in succeeding editions only compounded the confusion. I should note that logical organization had seldom been a strong point of previous cookbooks.

I should add that there already exists a facsimile edition of the work. *The Virginia Housewife: or Methodical Cook. By Mrs. Mary Randolph. Method is the Soul of Management.* Philadelphia: E. H. Butler & Co., 1860. Facsimile, New York: Avenel (Crown) with Valentine Museum, Richmond, n.d. [1970?]. Its only virtue lay in its existence, for which one must be grateful, but it is undoubtedly responsible for the persistence of the error regarding the year of publication.

APPENDIX II

Recipes that first appeared in *The Virginia House-wife. Method is the soul of management.* [By Mrs. Mary Randolph.] Second edition, with amendments and additions. Washington: 1825.

TO DRESS TURTLE

Kill it at night in winter, and in the morning in summer. Hang it up by the hind fins, cut off the head and let it bleed well. Separate the bottom shell from the top, with great care, lest the gall bladder be broken, which must be cautiously taken out and thrown away. Put the liver in a bowl of water. Empty the guts and lay them in water; if there be eggs, put them also in water. It is proper to have a separate bowl of water for each article. Cut all the flesh from the bottom shell, and lay it in water; then break the shell in two, put it in a pot after having washed it clean; pour on as much water as will cover it entirely, add one pound of middling, or flitch of bacon, with four onions chopped, and set it on the fire to boil. Open the guts, cleanse them perfectly; take off the inside skin, and put them in the pot with the shell; let them boil steadily for three hours, and if the water boils away too much, add more. Wash the top shell nicely after taking out the flesh, cover it, and set it by. Parboil the fins, clean them nicely—taking off all the black skin, and put them in water; cut the flesh taken from the bottom and top shell, in small pieces; cut the fins in two, lay them with the flesh in a dish; sprinkle some salt over, and cover them up. When the shell, &c. is done, take out the bacon, scrape the shell clean, and strain the liquor; which must be put back in the pot, about one quart of it; reserve the rest for soup; pick out the guts, and cut them in small pieces; take all the nice bits that were strained out, put them with the guts into the gravy; lay in the fins cut in pieces with them, and as much of the flesh as will be sufficient to fill the upper shell; add to it, (if a large turtle,) one bottle of white wine; cayenne pepper, and salt, to your taste; one gill of mushroom catsup, one gill of lemon pickle, mace, nutmegs and cloves, pounded, to season it high. Mix two large spoonsful of flour in one pound and a quarter of butter; put it in with thyme, parsley, marjoram and savory, tied in bunches; stew all these together, till the flesh and fins are tender; wash out the top shell, put a puff paste around the brim; sprinkle over the shell pepper and salt, then take the herbs out of the stew; if the gravy is not thick enough, add a little more flour, and fill the shell; should there be no eggs in the turtle, boil six new laid ones for ten minutes, put them in cold water a short time, peel them, cut them in two, and place them on the turtle; make a rich forcemeat, (see receipt for forcemeat,) fry the balls nicely, and put them also in the shell; set it in a dripping pan, with something under the sides to keep it steady; have the oven heated as for bread, and let it remain in it till nicely browned. Fry the liver and send it in hot.

FOR THE SOUP

At an early hour in the morning, put on eight pounds of coarse beef, some bacon, onions, sweet herbs, pepper and salt. Make a rich soup, strain it and thicken it with a bit of butter, and brown flour; add to it the water left from boiling the bottom shell; season it very high with wine, catsup, spice and cayenne; put in the flesh you reserved, and if that is not enough, add the nicest parts of a well boiled calf's head; but do not use the eyes or tongue; let it boil 'till tender, and serve it up with fried forcemeat balls in it.

If you have curry powder, (see receipt for it,) it will give a higher flavour to both soup and turtle, than spice. Should you not want soup, the remaining flesh may be fried, and served with a rich gravy.

TO BROIL CALF'S LIVER

Cut it in slices, put over it salt and pepper; broil it nicely, and pour on some melted butter with chopped parsely after it is dished.

BOLOGNA SAUSAGES

Take one pound of bacon—fat and lean, one ditto veal, do.—pork, do. suet, chop all fine, season highly—fill the skins, prick and boil them an hour, and hang them to dry—grated bread or boiled rice may be added; clean the skins with salt and vinegar.

COD FISH PIE

Soak the fish [*salt cod*], boil it and take off the skin, pick the meat from the bones and mince it very fine; take double the quantity of your fish of stale bread grated—pour over it as much new milk boiling hot, as will wet it completely—add minced parsley, nutmeg, pepper, and made mustard, with as much melted butter as will make it sufficiently rich; the quantity must be determined by that of the other ingredients:—beat these together very well, add the minced fish, mix it all, cover the bottom of the dish with good paste, pour the fish in, put on a lid [of pastry] and bake it.

TO DRESS ANY KIND OF SALTED FISH

Take the quantity necessary for the dish, wash them, and lay them in fresh water for a night, then put them on the tin plate with holes, and place it in the fish kettle—sprinkle over it pounded cloves and pepper with four cloves of garlic; put in a bundle of sweet herbs and parsley, a large spoonful of tarragon, and two of common vinegar, with a pint of wine; roll one quarter of a pound of butter in two spoonsful of flour, cut it in small pieces and put it over the fish—

cover it closely, and simmer it over a slow fire half an hour; take the fish out carefully, and lay it in the dish, set it over hot water, and cover it till the gravy has boiled a little longer—take out the garlic and herbs, pour it over the fish and serve it up. It is very good when eaten cold with salad, garnished with parsley.

TO FRICASSEE COD SOUNDS AND TONGUES

Soak them all night in fresh water, take off the skin, cut them in two pieces and boil them in milk and water till quite tender, drain them in a colander, and season with nutmeg, pepper, and a little salt—take as much new milk as will make sauce for it, roll a good lump of butter in flour, melt it in the milk, put the fish in, set it over the fire, and stir it till thick enough, and serve it up.

AN EXCELLENT WAY TO DRESS FISH

Dredge the fish well with flour, sprinkle salt and pepper on them, and fry them a nice brown; set them by to get cold; put a quarter of a pound of butter in a frying pan; when it boils, fry tomatas with the skins taken off, parsley nicely picked and a very little chopped onion; when done, add as much water as will make sauce for the fish—season it with pepper, salt, and pounded cloves, add some wine and mushroom catsup; put the fish in, and when thoroughly heated serve it up.

SPANISH METHOD OF DRESSING GIBLETS

Take the entrails of fat full grown fowls, empty them of their contents—open them with a sharp knife, scrape off the inner coat; wash them clean and put them on to boil with the liver, gizzard, and other giblets; add salt, pepper, and chopped onion—when quite tender set them by to cool; put some nice dripping or butter in a pan, when it boils put the giblets, add salt, fry them a nice brown; when nearly done, break six eggs in a bowl, beat them a little, pour them over the giblets, stir them for a few minutes and serve them up.

MOCK MACARONI

Break some crackers in small pieces, soak them in milk until they are soft; then use them as a substitute for macaroni.

PASTE FOR MEAT DUMPLINS

Chop half a pound of suet very fine—add one and a quarter pound of flour, and a little salt—mix it up with half a pint of milk, knead it till it tooks light; take a bowl of proper size, rub the inside with butter, roll out the paste and lay it in; parboil beef steaks, mutton-chops, or any kind of meat you like; season it and lay it in the bowl—fill it with rich gravy, close the paste over the top—get a very thick cloth that will keep out the water; wet and flour it, place it over the top of the bowl—gather it at bottom and tie it very securely; the water must boil when you put it in— when done, dip the top in cold water for a moment, that the cloth may not stick to the paste; untie and take it off carefully—put a dish on the bowl and turn it over—if properly made, it will come out without breaking; have gravy in a boat to eat with it.

OMELETTE—ANOTHER WAY

Break six eggs, leave out half the whites—beat them with a fork, and add some salt and chopped parsley; take four ounces of fresh butter, cut half of it in small pieces, put them in the omelette, put the other half in a small frying pan; when melted, pour in the eggs, stir till it begins to set, then turn it up round the edges; when done, put a plate on and turn the pan up, that it may not break—the omelette must be thick, and great care must be taken in frying: instead of parsley, you may use any kind of sweet herb, or onion chopped fine, anchovy minced, rasped beef, ham or tongue.

TO FRICASSEE EGGS

Boil six eggs for five minutes, lay them in cold water, peel them carefully, dredge them lightly with flour—beat one egg light, dip the hard eggs in, roll them in bread crumbs, seasoned with pepper, salt, and grated nutmeg; cover them well with this, and let them stand some time to dry—fry them in boiling lard, and serve them up with any kind of rich, well seasoned gravy, and garnish with crisped parsley.

TO SCOLLOP TOMATAS

Peel off the skin from large, full, ripe tomatas—put a layer in the bottom of a deep dish, cover it well with bread grated fine; sprinkle on pepper and salt, and lay some bits of butter over them—put another layer of each, till the dish is full—let the top be covered with crumbs and butter—bake it a nice brown.

TO STEW TOMATAS

Take off the skin, and put them in a pan with salt, pepper, and a large piece of butter—stew them till sufficiently dry.

AN APPLE CUSTARD

Pare and core twelve pippins—slice them tolerably thick—put a pound of loaf sugar in a stew pan, with a pint of water and twelve cloves; boil and skim it, then put in the apples, and stew them till clear, and but little of the syrup remains—lay them in a deep dish, and take out the cloves; when the apples are cold, pour in a quart of rich boiled custard—set it in water, and make it boil till the custard is set—take care the water does not get into it.

BOILED LOAF

Pour a quart of boiling milk over four little rolls of bread—cover them up, turning them occasionally 'till saturated with the milk—tie them very tight in cloths, and boil them an hour—lay them in the dish, and pour a little melted butter over them; for sauce, have butter in a boat, seasoned with wine, sugar and grated nutmeg.

TRANSPARENT PUDDING

Beat eight eggs very light, add half a pound of pounded sugar, the same of fresh butter melted, and half a nutmeg grated; sit it on a stove, and keep stirring 'till it is as thick as buttered eggs—put a puff paste in a shallow dish, pour in the ingredients, and bake it half an hour in a moderate oven—sift sugar over it, and serve it up hot.

FAYETTE PUDDING

Slice a loaf of bread tolerably thick—lay the slices in the bottom of a dish, cutting them so as to cover it completely; sprinkle some sugar and nutmeg, with a little butter, on each layer; when all are in, pour on a quart of good boiled custard sweetened—serve up cold.

MACCARONI PUDDING

Simmer half a pound of maccaroni in a plenty of water, with a table-spoonful of salt, till tender, but not broke—strain it, beat five yelks, two whites of eggs, half a pint of cream—mince white meat and boiled ham very fine, add three spoonsful of grated cheese, pepper and salt; mix these with the maccaroni, butter the mould, put it in, and steam it in a pan of boiling water for an hour—serve with rich gravy.

POTATO PASTE [Apple Dumplins]

Boil mealy potatos quite soft, first taking off the skins; rub them while hot through a sieve, put them in a stew pan over the fire, with as much water as will make it the consistence of thick mush; sift one quart of flour, and make it into a paste; with this mush, knead it till light, roll it out thin, make the dumplins small—fill them with apples, or any other fruit—tie them up in a thick cloth, and boil them nicely—eat them with butter, sugar, and nutmeg.

SPANISH FRITTERS

Make up a quart of flour, with one egg well beaten, a large spoonful of yeast, and as much milk as will make it a little softer than muffin dough; mix it early in the morning—when well risen, work in two spoonsful of melted butter; make it in balls the size of a walnut, and fry them a light brown in boiling lard— eat them with wine and sugar, or molasses.

SODA CAKES

Dissolve half a pound of sugar in a pint of milk; add a teaspoonful of soda, pour it on two pounds of flour— melt half a pound of butter, knead all together till light—pour it in shallow moulds, and bake it quickly in a brisk oven.

RICE BREAD

Boil six ounces of rice in a quart of water 'till it is dry and soft—put it into two pounds of flour, mix it in well; add two tea-spoonsful of salt, two large spoons- ful of yeast, and as much water as will make it the consistence of bread, when well risen—bake it in moulds.

MIXED BREAD

Put a tea-spoonful of salt, and a large one of yeast, into a quart of flour; make it sufficiently soft, with corn meal gruel; when well risen, bake it in a mould. It is an excellent bread for breakfast. Indifferent flour will rise much better, when made with gruel, than with fair water.

ANOTHER METHOD FOR MAKING YEAST

Peel one large Irish potatoe, boil it 'till soft, rub it through a sieve—add an equal quantity of flour, make it sufficiently liquid with hop tea; and when a little warmer than new milk, add a gill of good yeast—stir it well, and keep it closely covered in a small pitcher.

RICE BLANC MANGE

Boil a tea-cup full of rice in a very small quantity of water, 'till it is near bursting—them add half a pint of milk, boil it to a mush, stirring all the time—season it with sugar, wine, and nutmeg—dip the mould in water, and fill it; when cold, turn it in a dish, and surround it with boiled custard seasoned or syllabub—garnish it with marmalade.

CURRANT JELLY

Pick full ripe currants from the stem, and put them in a stone pot, then set it in an iron pot of water—take care that no water gets in: when the currants have yielded their juice, pour them into a jelly bag—let it run as long as it will without pressing, which must be reserved for the best jelly; you may then squeeze the bag to make inferior kind. To each pint of this juice, put one pound of loaf sugar powdered—boil it fifteen or twenty minutes—skim it clean and put it in glasses; expose them daily to the sun to prevent fermentation.

TOMATA SOY

Take a bushel of full ripe tomatas, cut them in slices without skinning—sprinkle the bottom of a large tub with salt, strew in the tomatas, and over each layer of about two inches thick, sprinkle half a pint of salt, and three onions sliced without taking off the skins.

When the bushel of tomatas is thus prepared, let them remain for *three* days, then put them into a large iron pot, in which they must boil from early in the morning 'till night, constantly stirring to prevent their sticking and mashing them.

The next morning, pass the mixture through a sieve, pressing it to obtain all the liquor you can; and add to it one ounce of cloves, quarter of a pound of allspice, quarter of a pound of whole black pepper, and a small wine glass of Cayenne; let it boil slowly and constantly during the whole of the day—in the evening, put it into a suitable vessel to cool, and the day after bottle and cork it well: place it in a cool situation during warm weather, and it will keep for many years, provided it has been boiled very slowly and sufficiently in the preparation. Should it ferment, it must be boiled a second time.

OBSERVATIONS ON PICKLING

The vessels for keeping pickles should be made of stone ware, straight from the bottom to the top, with stone covers to them; when the mouth is very wide, the pickles may be taken out without breaking them. The motive for keeping all pickles in plain vinegar previous to putting them in the prepared pot, is to draw off the water with which they are saturated, that they may not weaken the vinegar of the pot. The best way to dry all articles for the yellow pickle, is to take advantage of a clear hot day, and put them in full sun-shine on a table covered with a soft thick cloth, with the corners pinned securely that they may not blow up over the articles; the cloth absorbs the moisture, and by turning them frequently on a dry place, they become white and receive the colour of the turmeric more readily: one day of clear sun-shine is sufficient to prepare them for the first vinegar. Pickles keep much better when the vinegar is not boiled.

TO MAKE A SUBSTITUTE FOR ARRACK

Dissolve two scruples flowers of Benzoin, in one quart of good rum.

GINGER BEER

Pour two gallons of boiling water on two pounds brown sugar, one and a half ounce of cream of tartar, and the same of pounded ginger; stir them well, and put it in a small cask; when milk warm, put in half a pint of good yeast, shake the cask well, and stop it close—in twenty-four hours it will be fit to bottle, cork it very well, and in ten days it will sparkle like Champaigne: one or two lemons cut in slices and put in, will improve it much. For economy, you may use molasses instead of sugar—one quart in place of two pounds. This is a wholesome and delicious beverage in warm weather.

COLOGNE WATER

Three quarts spirits of wine, six drachms oil of lavender, one drachm oil of rosemary, three drachms essence of lemon, ten drops oil of cinnamon—mix them together very well.

TO DRY HERBS

Gather them on a dry day, just before they begin to blossom; brush off the dust, cut them in small branches, and dry them quickly in a moderate oven; pick off the leaves when dry, pound and sift them— bottle them immediately, and cork them closely. They must be kept in a dry place.

TO CLEAN TIN VESSELS

First wash off the grease, then scour them with fine sand and weak lie—rinse them with hot soap suds, and wipe them 'till dry.

APPENDIX III

Facsimile of designs for a home refrigerator and a tub, with accompanying explanations, as they appeared uniquely in the 1825 edition.

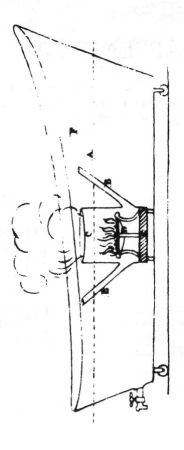

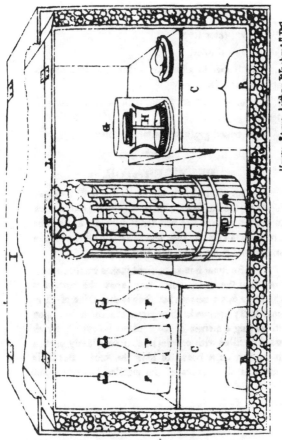

Howry Stone Lithing Washing" &c.

EXPLANATIONS OF THE PLATES.

BATH.

A. The water line.

C. The cylinder.

B. B. Tubes to admit air under the fire, and to serve as handles.

E. Double bottom filled with lead to keep it steady.

D. A tripod grate to contain the fire.

REFRIGERATOR.

A. The outer box must be strong and well put together, the lid fixed with strong hinges and a stick to hold it open in the manner of a Piano Forte; the dimensions must be four feet in length, three feet in width, and three and a half feet deep.

B. The inner box to be eight inches smaller every way than the outer one. Lay upon the bottom of the large box a smooth bed four inches thick of charcoal finely pounded, then place the inner box upon it, leaving a margin of four inches all round, which must be filled with powdered charcoal closely packed in; screw on a board to hide the coal. Put little pieces in the corners of the smaller box to support the inner lid about two inches below the top of the box. This lid must have a board six inches wide fixed with hinges to turn back lengthway, for the purpose of taking things out without raising the lid entirely, which would admit the warm air, and must only be done in the morning when the refrigerator is arranged for the day.

I. Outer lid.

L. Inner lid with part turned back.

E. Ice frame.

D. Tub to receive the water as the ice melts in the frame. The tub must be oval and of a convenient size to stand across the middle of the refrigerator, leaving room for a bench on each side.

C. C. Benches to hold bottles, &c.

F. F. F. Bottles in the bench C.

G. Tin bucket to hold a plate with a print of butter on it.

H. Tripod to stand over the plate in the bucket, and to hold another plate of butter without pressing the prints together.

K. Ice frame standing out of the tub to shew the legs that support it. It must be a little smaller than the tub, that the water may not run over the sides to wet the refrigerator. Lay a thick woollen cloth under the tub to absorb the moisture, and change it whenever the tub is emptied.

When the refrigerator first goes into operation, fill the ice frame to the top; raise the lids every morning, place in all the articles that are to be cooled, put in ice to supply the deficiency occasioned by melting, and when the tub is nearly full of water, empty it.

With judicious management it will require but little ice to keep up the quantity in the frame.

The refrigerator is more convenient than an ice house, for keeping both raw and cooked provisions; water melons, milk, butter, &c. &c. and for corning meat under the benches, in the hottest summer months.

APPENDIX IV

Recipes that first appeared in *The Virginia House-wife, or Methodical Cook*. By Mrs. Mary Randolph. Method is the soul of management. Third edition, with amendments and additions. Washington: 1828.

MOCK TURTLE SOUP OF CALF'S HEAD

Have a large head cleaned nicely without taking off the skin, divide the chop from the front of the head, take out the tongue, (which is best when salted,) put on the head with a gallon of water, the hock of a ham or a piece of nice pork, four or five onions, thyme, parsley, cloves and nutmeg, pepper and salt, boil all these together until the flesh on the head is quite tender, then take it up, cut all into small pieces, take the eyes out carefully, strain the water in which it was boiled, add half a pint of wine and a gill of mushroom catsup, let it boil slowly 'till reduced to two quarts, thicken it with two spoonsful of browned flour rubbed into four ounces of butter, put the meat in and after stewing it a short time, serve it up. The eyes are a great delicacy.

VEAL CUTLETS

Cut them from the fillet, put them in a stew pan with a piece of nice pork, a clove of garlic, a bundle of thyme and parsley, pepper and salt, cover them with water and let them stew ten or fifteen minutes, lay them on a dish, and when cold cover them well with the crumb of stale bread finely grated, mixed with the leaves of parsley chopped very small, some pepper, salt and grated nutmeg; press these on the veal with a knife, and when a little dried, turn it and do the same to the other side; put a good quantity of lard in a pan, when it boils lay the cutlets in carefully that the crumbs may not fall, fry them a little brown, lay them on a strainer to drain off the grease, do the same with the crumbs that have fallen in the pan; while this is doing simmer the water they were boiled in to half a pint, strain it and thicken it with four ounces of butter and a little browned flour; add a gill of wine and one of mushroom catsup, put in the cutlets and crumbs, and stew till tender; add forcemeat balls.

FRICASSEE OF SMALL CHICKENS

Take off the legs and wings of four chickens, separate the breasts from the backs, cut off the necks and divide the backs across, clean the gizzards nicely, put them with the livers and other parts of the chicken, after being washed clean, into a sauce pan, add pepper, salt, and a little mace, cover them with water, and stew them 'till tender, then take them out, thicken half a pint of the water with two table spoonsful of flour rubbed into four ounces of butter, add half a pint of new milk, boil all together a few minutes, then add a gill of white wine, stirring it in carefully that it may not curdle, put the chickens in and continue to shake the pan until they are sufficiently hot, and serve them up.

FRIED CHICKENS

Cut them up as for the fricassee, dredge them well with flour, sprinkle them with salt, put them into a good quantity of boiling lard, and fry them a light brown, fry small pieces of mush and a quantity of parsley nicely picked to be served in the dish with the chickens, take half a pint of rich milk, add to it a small bit of butter with pepper, salt, and chopped parsley, stew it a little, and pour it over the chickens, and then garnish with the fried parsley.

TO MAKE YELLOW PICKLE

Put all the articles intended for the yellow pickle in a pot, and pour on them boiling salt and water—let them stand forty-eight hours, take advantage of a clear hot day—press the water from the articles, and lay them to dry in full sunshine, on a table covered with a thick soft cloth, with the corners pinned securely, that they may not blow up over the things—

the cloth absorbs the moisture; and by turning them frequently on a dry place, they become white, and receive the colour of the turmeric more readily—one day of clear sunshine is enough to prepare them for the first vinegar. When dried, put them in a pot of plain cold vinegar, with a little turmeric in it—let them remain in it two weeks to draw off the water from them, and to make them plump—then put them in a clean pot, and pour on the vinegar, prepared by the following directions—this is the most economical and best way of keeping them—mix the turmeric very smoothly, before you add it to your pickles.

[In the 1828 edition, this recipe is followed by TO PREPARE VINEGAR FOR GREEN OR YELLOW PICKLE, for which see page 205 of the facsimile.]

TO MAKE GREEN PICKLES

Put the articles you intend to pickle in a pot and cover them with boiling salt and water, put a thick cloth on the top and then a plate that will fit it—let it stand 'till the next morning, then pour off the salt and water, boil it again, and cover them as before, do this until your pickles are a good green—then put them in plain cold vinegar, with some turmeric in it, and at the end of a fortnight, put them up, as you do the yellow pickle.

APPENDIX V*

Chart from *Thomas Jefferson's Garden Book, 1766–1824*

A STATEMENT OF THE VEGETABLE MARKET OF WASHINGTON, DURING A PERIOD OF 8 YEARS* WHEREIN THE EARLIEST & LATEST APPEARANCE OF EACH ARTICLE WITHIN THE WHOLE 8. YEARS IS NOTED.

Months across top: Feb. Mar. Apr. May June July Aug. Sep. Oct. Nov. Dec. Jan. Feb. Mar. Apr. May

Article	Earliest – Latest (noted dates)
Lettuce	
Parsley	
spinach	
sprouts	
corn salled	22 — 4 — 28
radishes	
sorrel	
asparagus	30 — 20
broccoli	31
cucumbers	3 — 6 — 7—24 — 23 — 26
cabbage	
strawberries	3 — 8
peas	9
turneps	30
potato Irish	1 — 9
snaps	5
artichokes	9 — 16
carrots	10
salsifia	11
raspberries	11 — 4
squashes	12 — 6
Windsor beans	16 — 6
beets	17
currants	29
parsneps	
watermelons	7 — 8 — 26
corn	16 — 22
tomatoes	16 — 16 — 20
melons	2 — 19
mushrooms	11 — 27
Limabeans	27 — 17
grapes	
endive	
celery	
eggplant	1 — 27
cauliflower	28 — 16 — 9 — 7
cresses	16 — 16

Other noted dates within the chart: 13 (Sep.), 27 (Oct.), 17 (Nov.), 11 / 30 (Dec.), 18 (Oct.), 18 (Mar.), 16 / 8 (Apr.), 15 (Mar.), 21 (Apr.), 28 (Feb.).

*These eight years involved are those of Thomas Jefferson's terms of presidency: 1801–1809

(Randall, *Jefferson* 1: pl. facing p. 44.)

Historical Glossary

A-LA-DAUBE and A-LA-MODE—In France, *la daube* is a rustic dish of meat braised for hours on end with wine, pork rind, and aromatics; beef is understood but any meat too tough for roasting is a fair subject. It is normally served hot. *Boeuf à la mode* is a refined version from classic cuisine; calf's foot replaces pork rind and more emphasis is placed on presentation, which is typically cold.

Both terms showed up in English cookbooks by early eighteenth century. The dishes tended to be pale versions of French recipes and any differentiation was inconsistent; beef was virtually invariable.

Amelia Simmons held to the English view in this regard but Mrs. Randolph had a different understanding. She used *a-la-daube* to designate a presentation dish in separately made sparkling jelly (see *Savoury Jelly*, facsimile) with little or no relationship to either French or English practice of her time. I find no primary documentation on *la daube glacée* of French Creole cuisine until late nineteenth century, but the *daube* brought to the New World by the French clearly stems from a much earlier period. French seventeenth-century recipes show a surprising range of choice of subject, with goose and turkey being perhaps the most common. All call for braising in a rich liquid that expressly jells on cooling, and many are served cold. L. Liger, in *Dictionaire Pratique du Bon Ménager de Campagne et de Ville* (1715) defines *daube* as "a ragout which is eaten cold and which is much in use today," but sometime during the century it fell from favor in classical cuisine, surviving in the provinces in various forms. French Creoles used the term with careless abandon; *daube de poisson* (see *Fish a-la-daub*, facsimile) and even *daube de bananes* show up in the Antilles, for example. So that Mrs. Randoph's six *a-la-daube* recipes clearly have French Creole inspiration. As suggested earlier, her *Beef a-la-mode* may have come from French sources.

ALKANET—The root of *Anchusa* or *Alkanna tinctoria* (as well as certain other members of the borage family) gives a fine red dye that has been in recorded use for centuries. The name comes from Arab *al-henna,* the ancient cosmetic dye.

APOQUINIMINC CAKES—These are beaten biscuits, often called Maryland biscuits. I find it difficult to account for the Indian name; the ingredients are English as is the technique of beating dough for tenderness; Thomas Dawson in *The Good Huswifes Jewell* (1586), for example, calls for beating dough for sweet *bisket bread* with "a slyce of Wood" for two hours.

ARRACK—The name comes from Arabic *araq*, meaning juice, and spread throughout the East, coming to refer to virtually any local fermented drink. The *arrack*, or *rack*, of the American colonists, originally imported from British India or the Dutch East Indies, was based on rum flavored with various Eastern flowers or spices *(OED, Webster)*.

Flowers of Benzoin come from the benjamin bush or spice bush *(Lindera benzoin* Meissn. *Laurineae)*, according to Sturtevant. He cites early use of the berries as a substitute for allspice, for instance.

BELL FRITTERS—These are *beignets*, or French doughnuts; the dough is that also used for cream puffs. There is an identical recipe for *Bell Fritters* in the Martha Jefferson Randolph collection which is attributed to Le Maire, Jefferson's *maître d'hôtel* at the White House. The name refers to the shape.

BOLOGNA—This English sausage early lost whatever resemblance it may have once had to *mortadella*. The basic proportions given by Mrs. Glasse in 1755 are identical to those in Mrs. Randolph's recipe.

BREADS—The recipe *To Make Bread* (facsimile) harks back to the *manchet*, the individual loaf or large roll made of finest flour that constituted the daily bread of upper-class England from perhaps the fourteenth century through the seventeenth, or thereabouts. In fact, the dough for manchet differed little if at all from that for fine white bread or the later rolls; my comment is prompted by Mrs. Randolph's assumption in her only recipe for wheat bread that it be baked in rolls rather than large loaves, a telling note. The upper-class origins of so many Virginia colonists may account for this historical preference for individual loaves; great loaves were associated with peasants and the poor.

These rolls were made on the overnight sponge system and meant to be cast and baked on the floor of a brick oven. The proportions of only ten ounces of water to twenty of flour, even the relatively soft Virginia flour, makes a stiffish dough (see *flour, weights & measures,* and *yeast,* for additional information).

The *French Rolls* (facsimile) represent an *English* usage that dates back at least to the late thirteenth century; that is, the recipe does not purport to present contemporary French practice (I comment on these enriched breads at some length in *Martha Washington's Booke of Cookery.*)

The recipes for *Muffins* (facsimile) and for *Crumpets* (facsimile) are perfectly traditional English recipes that remained popular in America until they were displaced by baking powder versions later in the century.

Recipes for *Rice Bread (Appendix II)* were highly popular in nineteenth-century cookbooks, especially in the South. Rice bread is delicious and should be revived. *Sweet Potato Buns* (facsimile) are sweet buns made with white potato. Mrs. Randolph always specified sweet potato when so intended (see *Sweet-Potato Pudding*, for example). Similar rolls made with sweet potato came to be a Virginia specialty, however, so that a case may be made for either.

Batter Bread (facsimile) is often described as a synonym for spoon bread and indeed recipes for the two are ill-differentiated. But Mrs. Randolph's recipe is akin to that for *Puff Pudding* (facsimile), actually popovers or tiny Yorkshire puddings; the only difference is the addition of a little cornmeal in the batter bread. Later recipes for spoon bread, and batter bread as well, came to call for separately beaten egg yolks and whites added to cornmeal mush and milk; the ingredients are nearly identical but the change in method produces a spongy texture quite unlike that of Mrs. Randolph's batter bread.

Chocolate Cakes (facsimile) are to accompany the beverage, as coffee cake. I do not find use of chocolate or cocoa in cakes until after mid-nineteenth century in American cookbooks.

For *Apoquiniminc Cakes, Journey,* or *Johnny Cake* and cornmeal breads, and *cassada bread,* see glossary.

BROCCOLI—John Evelyn refers to "The *Broccoli* from *Naples*" in *Acetaria: A Discourse of Sallets* (1699), and recipes for it appear with increasing frequency thereafter. Beginning in 1767, Jefferson routinely notes plantings of several varieties of broccoli and it was sold in the Washington market during his years of presidency (see *Appendix V*). None of this is arcane, yet food writers regularly place its introduction to the American food scene in the 1920s.

Broccoli is *Brassica oleracea* var. *botrytis;* the stalky type mentioned by Mrs. Randolph may be *broccoli di rapa,* variety of *Brassica Napus* with green florets, to be found in Italian neighborhoods.

CASSADA BREAD—*Cassada (Manihot utilissima),* from Haitian Taino, is also variously known as *mandioc, yuca,* and more familiar to us, *tapioca,* a prepared form of the flour. The earliest mention I find of cassava bread in North America is in *A Report of the New Found Land in Virginia* by Thomas Hariot (1588):

"*Coscúshaw,* some of our company tooke to bee that kinde of roote which the Spaniards in the West Indies call *Cassavy,* whereupon also many called it by that name: it groweth in very muddie pooles and moist groundes. Being dressed according to the countrey maner, it maketh a good bread, and also a good spoonemeate, and is used very much by the inhabitants: The juice of this root is poison, and therefore heede must be taken before anything be made therewithall: Either the rootes must bee first sliced and dried in the Sunne, or by the fire, and then being pounded into floure wil make good bread: or els while they are greene they are to be pared, cut into pieces and stampt; loves of the same to be laid neere or over the fire untill it be soure, and then being well pounded again, bread, or spoone meate very god in taste, and holsome may be made thereof."

(The use of *spoonemeate,* an old English term for soft food, suggests a possible association with Southern *spoon bread.*)

I do not know how long cassava bread survived in Virginia as I am unable to find other references, let along recipes. (Jefferson simply lists cassava as an indigenous plant.) Perhaps Mrs. Randolph was evoking an already dying tradition in 1824 when she lovingly likened it to her johnny cake (facsimile). Indeed, one may speculate that the little known early presence of cassava bread in the South influenced the choice of rice over Indian meal in Southern recipes for *johnny cake.*

CATSUP—The word comes from Amoy *kētsiap* or Malay *kēchap,* meaning brine of pickled shellfish; forms of the word appear in English by 1690, according to *OED.* The English had long used anchovies and pickled oysters as condiments (harking back to the *garum* of ancient Rome), so that their swift adoption of the name and new variations is not surprising.

Mrs. Rundell's recipe for *Tomata Sauce* in 1814 may be the earliest printed recipe for tomato catsup. Until nearly mid-century in America, *catsup* was generally understood to be based on mushrooms or walnuts. (See also *soy.*)

CAVEACH—Name and dish come from the Arabs (*iskebêŷ,* to pickle with vinegar, according to Corominas) by way of Spanish *escabeche. OED* assigns a West Indian origin to *caveach* (a corruption of *esca-*

beche), a name which did not become current until mid-eighteenth in England. But recipes for the dish, the characterizing note of which is dusting with flour and frying in olive oil before pickling, had long been known in England. A highly detailed recipe, *To pickle mackrell, Flounders, Soles, or Sprats*, appears in *Martha Washington's Booke of Cookery* (about 1650, or earlier) and is a perfectly classic *escabeche;* virtually no eighteenth-century cookbook is without similar recipes. In 1796, Mrs. Glasse presents *The Jews Way of preserving Salmon, and all Sorts of Fish,* also a true *escabeche;* it is possible that Jews fleeing the Inquisition had brought the recipe from Spain to England. But the dish had long before penetrated France, showing up as *espimbeche de rougets* in *Le Ménagier de Paris* (about 1393); name and dish persist in regional cookery to this day, demonstrating once again the difficulties of pinning down details of diffusion of a dish.

Caveach fell from favor in American cookbooks, disappearing altogether by the time of Fannie Farmer (1896). A pity, because it represents a particularly successful way of holding highly perishable fish for some days, actually heightening flavor. Home canning and ice boxes were responsible for this neglect, and gastronomic quality suffered, an ironic note. Of late, the dish has been rediscovered as *escabeche,* en item in "gourmet" exotica, another ironic note. With modern refrigeration, the pickling may be as mild as pleases you.

CHAFING DISH—This is the ancient *chafing dish of coals,* a charcoal brazier mounted on a tripod, varying in size from table top models to the large one specified by Mrs. Randolph for preserving. By varying the fuel, one could obtain surprising flexibility, and their use permitted fussy bits of cookery that would not have been possible at the fireplace. The *brick stove* that she mentions is a table height structure with hollowed out fire chambers topped with grills, a permanent chafing dish, in effect.

CHOWDER, A SEA DISH—The name and its application to fishermen's stew come from France. Versions of *la chaudrée* (*chaudron,* cauldron) are common along the coast from just north of Bordeaux well up into Brittany, where they merge with related dishes beginning with *la cotriade* (*côte,* coast). In 1789, Mrs. Glasse gives a recipe *To make Chouder, A Sea Dish:* cod, pickled pork, onions, [sea] biscuit, and water (it got fancied up in later editions). The key word is *sea* dish. I am convinced that English seamen learned of the dish from French seamen on early voyages to the fishing banks; the extent of mutual borrowing in their sea chanteys is remarkable, according to Barbara Scott. Salt pork and sea biscuit, still pretty much the hallmark of a proper chowder, would have been a typical sea cook's adaptation of French shore versions. Cookery of the humble has always been ill-recorded; Mrs. Glasse was unusual in that she recorded a number of *sea dishes,* and I believe that chowder had long been known in English fishing ports, perhaps for centuries, as well as in New England and Newfoundland later on. *OED* cites a 1552 recording by Strype of "fisher, or jowtar" (a variant of *chowder*) in Cornwall; the word, in various forms, survived as a term for fish hawker in Cornwall and neighboring Devon, both maritime counties (*OED* and Halliwell). It should be noted that the Cornish had close ties with the Bretons, fellow Celts who had fled Britain in the wake of Anglo-Saxon invasions of the fifth century, giving the Armorican peninsula their own name meaning *Britannia minor.* The plains of Cornouaille (pronounced *Cornwall,* or nearly) lie on the north side and *cornouaillais* is one of the principal dialects to this day, according to le Quid, *Bretagne* (Paris: Laffont, 1981). I am deeply indebted to Paula Cianci of the *Services Culturels de l'Ambassade de France* in New York for this documentation. In *Gastronomie Bretonne d'Hier et d'Aujourd'hui* (1965), the researcher Simone Morand gives a recipe for *Cotriade Cornouaillaise,* for instance.

One would like to believe the Quebec Indian claim of having originated chowder, the serendipitous meeting of Micmac cookery and French trappers toting their *chaudrons*. But coastal Indians steamed clams in sand pits lined with hot stones and seaweed—a clambake, which *is* Indian—or used other forms of "stone boiling." And not one characterizing auxiliary element of chowder is indigenous to the New World. (Potatoes and tomatoes are nineteenth-century additions, as is milk.) Clam chowder is nothing but a sometime substitution of clams for cod in the *sea dish;* after all, Europeans had been gathering and stewing various bivalves for millennia.

Mrs. Randolph's recipe amounts to an elegant variation on the 1789 recipe of Mrs. Glasse. Later Southern Recipes for chowder are not all that common and it is often described as a New England dish.

CIMLIN, CYMLING—Robert Beverley mentions these scalloped squash in 1705, saying that they "are sometimes call'd Cymnels . . . from the Lenten Cake of that Name, which many of them very much resemble." (*Cymling* is a variant of *simnel*.) They are better known outside of the South as *pattypan* squash, again from their shape. All early Virginia writers mention them; Jefferson classified them as *Cucurbita verrucosa*. (See *pumpkins and squash*.)

COCHINEAL—This is the dried bodies of the insect *Coccus cacti,* primarily from Mexico. It gives a brilliant scarlet dye and is used in medicine as an antispasmodic.

CORN MEAL, INDIAN MEAL—White cornmeal is often referred to in nineteenth-century Southern cookbooks but this is inconclusive; indeed, it suggests a choice. In answer to my question concerning the color of cornmeal in early Virginia, Patricia A. Gibbs, Research Assistant at Colonial Williamsburg Foundation, writes: "Considering that corn was the staple crop of colonial Virginia, it is particularly vexing that its color is seldom noted." The best primary reference, she says, is: "William Stephen's 25 July 1738 letter, written from Savannah to the Trustees of the Colony of Georgia in England," in which he complains that they did not have "a sufficient quantity of what they call Virginia Corn, which is large, broad, and white, and usually proves well here. . . ." This was in contrast to "a parcell of Yellow skinned Corn bought, highly commended for its usual increase in the Northern Provinces; but twas too fatally experienced that it proved very different here where the soil is not so cool a nature as when it grew before. . . ." [Great Britain, Public Record Office, C.O. 5/640, f. 140] (My thanks to Miss Gibbs for this information.)

Even Thomas Jefferson rarely mentions corn color, but he did note plantings of both yellow and white strains of "forward corn," one a "Maryland forward corn (white)," in 1794. It may be that early strains of yellow corn fared better than later ones, or his plantings may have been experimental.

Certainly white cornmeal is largely the rule in the South today, just as yellow is more common in the North, and Mrs. Randolph may not have felt it necessary to specify. (A notable exception in the North is the white cornmeal of Rhode Island, claimed to be an old Indian strain; it is of exceptional quality.)

In her *Kitchen Companion* (1887), Maria Parloa gives an illuminating explanation of why early recipes involving corn meal do not always work. I abridge:

The old process of making corn meal was to take corn which had dried naturally for a few months, and crush it between mill-stones. This gave a sweet-flavored but uneven meal. . . . As the corn was not entirely free of moisture, and was heated in being crushed between the mill-stones, it could not be relied upon to keep good; a few weeks was as long a time as it was expected to remain sweet. It is to be regretted that this delicious meal has passed away.

About fifteen or twenty years ago [1867–72] the granulated meal began to appear in the market. It was sweet, dry, and of even texture, being cut instead of being ground between stones. The corn was thoroughly dried before being sent to the mill; at first it was kept for two or three years, until all the moisture had evaporated. . . . If the manufacturers had been content to follow this process up to the present time, housekeepers would have been well pleased; but the drying of the corn was not rapid enough for the millers, who soon began to use kilns. . . . [They gradually increased the temperatures to shorten drying time and ground the meal finer, as well.] All these changes in the meal have damaged it considerably, and it is almost impossible to get the moist, sweet corn-bread of years gone by. If in using old receipts for corn bread, one-eighth of the quantity of meal called for be omitted, the bread will be nearer what should be than it will if all the meal be used.

What was true in 1887 has not bettered. However, water-ground meal of superior quality can be found by searching out traditional millers. The provenance and style of milling make all the difference.

DOUGH NUTS—A YANKEE CAKE—Bits of yeast dough fried in boiling oil are nearly universal—the

honeyed *loucoumades* of the Greeks, for example—
but *doughnuts* are associated with the Dutch in
America. (Mrs. Randolph's recipes for *Dough Nuts*
and *Spanish Fritters* differ only in detail, for example.) Washington Irving speaks of "balls of sweetened
dough, fried in hog's fat, and called doughnuts, or
olykoeks [properly *oliebollen,* dough balls cooked in
oil]". (*Knickerbocker's History of New York,* 1809; see
also *doughnuts* and *crullers.*)

I cannot date the shift of designation of *doughnut*
from these nut-shaped cakes to those with a hole;
recipes from the period abound but are usually mad-
deningly uninformative as to shape. In 1871, *Mrs.
Porter's New Southern Cookery Book* gives five recipes
for doughnuts and three for crullers; one in each cate-
gory calls for shapes in the form of a ring, coiled by
hand. By 1883, Mrs. Lincoln refers to a *doughnut
cutter.* But the shape was not new; various coiled and
ring-shaped fried cakes had been made for centuries
in the market places of the Middle East and Europe,
and for reason: proportionately more surface is ex-
posed to the boiling fat and the problem of soggy centers is obviated. Spanish *churros,* early crullers, and
funnel cakes come immediately to mind, and there
are various ancient scalded and baked breads such as
la rioute of Savoy and the *bagel* that have always been
ring-shaped.

I propose that the change of form of the *doughnut*
was imposed by the new baking powder doughs (see
pearl ash). Yeast doughs are wonderfully maniable;

in one swift continuous motion, you can pinch off a bit and throw it into the boiling fat, and even fanciful forms are easily worked. But baking powder doughs must be rolled and shaped and the problem of soggy centers is more severe. Sometime after mid-century, an ingenious and enterprising tinsmith must have devised a cutter that cut ring-shaped cakes in one stroke.

DUTCH OVEN—Until the kitchen range came into use, this capacious, relatively shallow, footed iron pot served not only as oven in humble homes, but as a surprisingly flexible and efficient auxiliary to the brick oven of the wealthy. This is in addition to its more familiar function as a braising pot. The pot was nestled in the embers, with embers or live coals piled in the rimmed lid (depending on the degree of heat desired), so that heat was well distributed for braising or baking bread. (As late as the 1853 edition of *Domestic Cookery*, Elizabeth Lea gives specific directions on how to bake bread in a Dutch oven, as well as in the new-fangled stove and the preferred brick oven.) In order to brown food, recipes sometimes called for placing it under the super-heated cover.

The term occasionally appeared in English cookbooks, as well. Since these pot ovens were of ancient and continuing use in England, as elsewhere, I cannot account for the sobriquet of *Dutch* except to suggest that it may have alluded to mythical Dutch frugality (as in *Dutch treat*) rather than to actual

Dutch or German infiltration, necessarily. (See also *tin Dutch oven.*)

EGGPLANT—This plant *(Solanum Melongina)* apparently came to Virginia from Africa as part of the slave trade; Byrd casually mentions *Guinea melons* (*Guinea squash* was more customary but terms were loose) in 1737. In any event, Jefferson frequently speaks of them and they were sold in the Washington market by the opening of the nineteenth century at least (see *Appendix V*), whatever has been written to the contrary. Eggplant is not African in origin but had been brought from the East by the Arabs; the name *aubergine* comes from Arabic *al-bâdindjân* by way of Catalan *alberginia (Robert)*. In 1597, Gerard noted that the *Madde Apple* (from Latin *Mala insana*) bore fruit "of the bigness of a Swans egge," so that its name in English becomes comprehensible, especially as it was often white, as noted by Mrs. Randolph.

FIELD PEAS—This legume is variously called *cornfield pea, cowpea, black-eye pea* or *bean,* among other names. A member of *Vigna sinensis,* it is technically neither pea nor bean, although the seed resembles a bean in appearance and use. It was brought to our South from Africa as part of the slave trade and has remained a pillar of southern cookery, black and white, ever since. Mrs. Randolph's recipe for them seems to be the first recorded one although early writers mention them, and Jefferson planted them regularly.

FLOUR—The technology for turning the golden life-giving wheat flour of yesteryear into the chalky life-less dust of today had not yet been perfected in the day of Mrs. Randolph. The wheat germ was still pretty much intact and even tiny flecks of bran escaped the bolting cloths, so that white flour was a lovely cream color and was more flavorful and nutritious than the flour of today. It was not until the 1870s that sugar was added to bread dough because the yeasts did not readily thrive in the "new process" flours that were taking over. Mrs. Lincoln (1883) was defensive about the practice: "Many object to the use of sugar in bread. Flour in its natural state contains sugar; this sugar is changed in fermentation. *Just enough sugar to restore the natural sweetness,* but not enough to give a really sweet taste, is necessary in fermented bread." [*Emphasis added.*] What she remembered, of course, was the sweet nutty flavor of old style milled flour. (She proposed a tablespoon to a batch; Fannie Farmer was to more than double that amount.)

The flour that Mrs. Randolph bought was not aged, judging by instructions in her recipe for bread (fac-simile). As noted elsewhere, southern flours were usually rather soft (see *breads* and *weights & measures*). Ideally, one ought to search out rather soft white flours from organic sources for these recipes; at the very least, use only *unbleached* and *unbromated* flour. Wholewheat flours do not appear to have been popular in Virginia, at least not among the gentry; later in the century, one does come across an occasional recipe calling for graham flour.

Among other flours and grains referred to by Mrs.

Randolph we find: *cornmeal,* oats, buckwheat, hominy, rice, sago, arrowroot, and *cassava.*

FLUMMERY—Traditionally it was a gelatinous sweet dish made by soaking oat grits but by 1747, Mrs. Glasse was giving recipes for flummery using gelatine from hartshorn.

FONDUS—These are actually *gougères* or cheese puffs, as may be seen.

FORCEMEAT BALLS—*Force* comes from French *farce,* stuffing; its use has characterized English cooking since medieval times. Mrs. Randolph's recipe (facsimile) is archetypically English.

FRENCH BEANS, SNAPS, and STRING BEANS—These comprise a distinct branch of *Phaseolus vulgaris,* to which the kidney bean of undisputed American origin also belongs, thus logically placing their origin in the New World as well. The reader should know, however, that no question of botanical classification and history is thornier than that of the legumes we loosely call beans. The writings of antiquity are not always precise and the earliest explorers knew little botany, meanwhile disseminating various seeds hither and yon in an immensely accelerated spread of plants, so that even the early encounter of a plant in a specific area by a trained observer is not in itself proof of long cultivation, much less of its being indigenous; the Indians, by all accounts, were quick to cultivate new plants and were apt gardeners. (This historical phenomenon also characterizes the history of *pumpkins and squash* and possibly *potatoes,* which see.) In brief, botanists are in disagreement.

The sobriquet of *French beans* in English was in counterdistinction to the older *English beans,* or broad beans (see *Mazagan beans*); the French must have early developed improved strains of edible pod kidney beans, *haricots verts.* (*Green beans* in English indifferently referred to either English or French edible pod beans.) There is a recipe, *To pickle kidney beans* in *Martha Washington's Booke of Cookery* (before 1650) that directs the reader to "string them very well," and to scald them until they "be greene & tender," which indicates early acceptance in England. (The term kidney bean was used by Turner in 1548, and the early chroniclers had all remarked on the shape of the mature bean seed.)

What is certain is that snap beans were early cultivated in Virginia. Byrd in 1737 mentions *French beans,* listing them among European beans as distinguished from *Indian beans.* Jefferson planted them regularly and noted when they first came to table, for example.

(Also, see *field peas* and *lima beans.*)

GUMBO, GOMBO, GUMBS—This name for *Hibiscus esculentus* comes from Angolan *kingombo; okra,* another popular name, is thought to come from West African *nkru-ma (OED).* The vegetable seems to have come to Virginia from black Africa, where it had long been cultivated, by way of the West Indies: Sir Hans Sloane reported in 1707 that *Ocra* was flourishing in Jamaica *(OED)*, and Mrs. Randolph herself describes *Gumbs* (*Gumbo* in later editions) as a "West Indian Dish" (facsimile). Jefferson makes no mention of okra until 1809 that I can find, but he planted it regularly thereafter.

Mrs. Randolph's *Gumbs* is simply buttered okra; her recipe for *Ochra Soup* (facsimile) more nearly resembles later recipes for gumbo, however. In 1847, Sarah Rutledge gives a recipe in *The Carolina Housewife* for *New Orleans Gumbo* calling for turkey, beef, water, onions, and oysters, to be made "mucilaginous [by stirring in] two spoonsful of pulverized sassafrasleaves." Clearly, the mucilaginous quality of gumbo had become its chief characteristic, so much so that we find *gumbo* applied to soups all over the South that typically did not include okra but were instead thickened with Creole *filé* (meaning thready), the powdered sassafras leaves that were still being gathered and sold by Indians at the turn of our century, according to Célestine Eustis in *Cooking in Old Créole Days* (1904). She describes *gombo* as an Indian festival dish that could be made with virtually any game or domestic bird, veal, etc., or combination thereof. *Gombomêlé*, a delightful Creole word, is figuratively used to denote a tremendously complex and tangled affair, she says. *Gumbo,* with its fascinating strands of black, Indian, and French influences, illustrates the delightful problem of tracing the history of a dish: *un gombomêlé*.

I should note, perhaps, that *gumbo* continued to

refer to the vegetable itself as well; *okra* remained aloof from the dual nature of *gumbo*.

HEN'S NEST—This is one of many conceits that were popular in English cookery of the eighteenth century, and earlier; Mrs. Glasse (1796) gives a similar recipe for *Hen's Nest*, and others for *Fish-Pond, Mouse Trap, Moon and Stars in Jelly*, etc.

ISINGLASS—This is leaf gelatine made from the bladder of the sturgeon. It is of high quality, somewhat less concentrated than our common granulated gelatine, of which ¾ ounce (3 packages) is more than ample for the liquid (3 pints) in Mrs. Randolph's recipe. (Soften the gelatine in ½ cup of cool water, then add 1 quart of boiling water and milk, stirring; continue the recipe. The overnight procedure is unnecessary.

JOURNEY, OR JOHNNY CAKE—The names, virtually alternative forms, I take to refer to the ease with which a handful of meal may be mixed with water and baked in cakes under summary conditions. I believe that both names came from England; popular forms have never been well recorded and their survival in the Colonies is altogether typical. In Australia, for instance, *johnny-cake* refers to a cake of wheatmeal baked in ashes or fried in a pan, according to *OED*. Some writers propose *Shawnee cake* but in the land of the Shawnees, large stretches of the South, Indian *pone* was the more usual name for cornmeal cakes while johnny cake was customarily made of rice (see *Rice Journey, or Johny Cake*, page 138 of facsimile, and *cassada bread*). It has been brought to my attention by John Thorne that Stuart Berg Flexner in *I Hear America Talking* (1979) suggests a derivation from "*joniken,* an Indian dish of flat, thin cornmeal cakes fried in grease" (on the order of Rhode Island *johnny cakes,* I suppose); no documentation is given. I find no mention of Indian fried bread in any early account (nor of frying, for that matter). And William Wood, in a remarkable bilingual *Nomenclator* in *New Englands Prospect* (1634), gives *petuc quanocke* and *isattananeise* as local Indian names for bread. Whatever the derivation of *johnny cake,* the colonists thought that it was *journey cake.*

OED cites from *A Concise History of East and West Florida* by Bernard Romans (1775): "Notwithstanding [rice] is . . . only fit for puddings . . . or to make the water-like bread called johnny cakes in Carolina."

The earliest recipe that I find is for *Johny Cake, or Hoe Cake* in *American Cookery* (1796) by Amelia Simmons. It calls for *Indian meal,* as do all New England recipes, and is "baked before the fire," presumably spread on a propped up hoe, plank, or stone (the ageless procedure described by Mrs. Randolph), as the colonists had been doing all along.

It must be understood that among the scores of johnny cakes, pones, ash cakes, hoe cakes, bannocks, and even various fried cakes, differentiation was not rigorous. Each colony, each community, had its own versions and names, a tradition that faded as the iron kitchen range made all hearth cakes virtually obsolete, except perhaps in Rhode Island where questions of choice of cornmeal, additions or no, and texture of their fried *jonny cakes* still stir lively interest. (It is this diversity and far-flung distribution that argue for the *journey cake* derivation.) Inevitably, the nomadic versions of meal and water came to be enriched in ways that varied from one community to another, compounding questions of differentiation further still.

Miss Rutledge gives a recipe for *Rice Journey, or Johnny Cake* in *The Carolina Housewife* (1847), as well as one for *Corn Journey, or Johnny Cake,* but the very name became curiously rare in southern cookbooks after that although all manner of quick breads of cornmeal, and even rice, continued.

JUMBALS—Mrs. Randolph is most uninformative as to procedure. Traditionally, the dough is rolled out like a cookie dough, cut into thin strips which are then twisted into various knotted forms, some not so different from a pretzel or a figure 8, for example; later, simple circlets were more common. English recipes go back to the sixteenth century; there are several in *Martha Washington's Booke of Cookery.*

LIMA, or SUGAR BEANS—These legumes are members of *Phaseolus lunatus* var. *macrocarpus,* according to Hawkes, and were cultivated by the pre-Columbian Incas. By Jefferson's day, at least, they were widely grown in Virginia.

MANGOS—In English cookery, *mango* is mock pickled mangoes, for which the English had developed a taste through imports from India. By 1699, recipes for making *Mango of Cucumbers* and one of walnuts appear in John Evelyn's *Acetaria: A Discourse of Sallets;* all eighteenth-century writers included recipes using various fruits such as peaches and small green melons. The invariable stuffing was part of the masquerade.

MAZAGAN BEANS—These are broad beans *(Vicia faba),* a staple of the Old World variously known as *fève, fava, faba,* and *fool* around the Mediterranean, where they are as old as time. With maturity, the individual bean coverings become very tough and must be removed; the entire pod is rarely eaten (but see *beans*). They were more commonly referred to as Windsor beans, and were grown by Jefferson early on; also, see *Appendix V.*

MOLASSES—Miss Parloa in 1887, complained that, "Now that sugar is finally boiled in vacuum pans, the best quality of molasses is very scarce. The finest comes from Porto Rico, and the next best from New Orleans." The situation has not improved since.

OKRA, OCHRA, OCRA—See *gumbo.*

PEARL ASH—This was a popular name for potassium carbonate, a refined form of potash, in turn an alkaline substance obtained by leaching ashes of wood or other plants *(pot ashes).* The use of wood ash in meat curing is ancient. And lye, the leaching water, has long been used for cleansing and making of soap.

But the use of these alkaline substances as leavening appears to be American in origin. Study of Indian lore is frustrating because of early contamination, but it does seem that Indians employed ash as seasoning because of its salt content, and as a foaming agent in their breads. With corn meal, even using purer forms, the effect is largely a change in texture; with wheat flour, the leavening is spectacular and virtually instantaneous, particularly when sparked by the acidity of sour milk, for example.

This usage is first recorded, it seems, in 1796 by Amelia Simmons in a recipe for gingerbread; molasses supplies the requisite acidity. But the practice clearly was widespread and already of long standing as shown by a recipe for *Handy-Cake or Bread* in *Essays and Notes on Husbandry and Rural Affairs* by J. B. Bordley (1801): "The good people of Long Island call this pot-ash or handy-cake; . . . wheaten flour 2 lbs; sugar ½ lb, have added to them a tea spoonful of salt of tartar heaped, or any other form of pot or pearl ash." All is moistened with a pint of milk, "the better if the milk is sour or coagulated," and enriched with ½ pound of butter if liked. So that housewives already understood that added acid improves the leavening action, that the cake must be "baked briskly" and immediately in order to be light, and that "More of potash than is allowed by the rule, would give an alkaline taste," something less well understood today.

Gradually, saleratus and other "baking sodas" replaced pearl ash; the ingredients called for in Mrs. Randolph's recipe for *Soda Cakes (Appendix II)* are otherwise identical to those in the Bordley recipe. Eventually, acid and alkali were combined in one "baking powder."

PEPPER—The word is made to do for two entirely different species: 1. *Piper nigrum* from the East Indies, the berry of which is our common black pepper corn (or white or green, depending on treatment), and was known in England since antiquity. 2. The *Capsicum* tribe, native to tropical America, which may be divided into two broad categories: mild and hot. Only mentions of *Capsicum* require comment.

Bell pepper is a large, fleshy mild green pepper, turning to red or gold when fully ripe. Sturtevant cites Lionel Wafer in 1699, who mentions *Bell-pepper* and *Bird-pepper* as growing in the *Isthmus of America,* and Edward Long in 1774, who lists nine varieties of *Capsicum* as being under cultivation in Jamaica; of these, "the Bell is esteemed most proper for pickling," Sturtevant repeats. Among numerous references to *Capsicum* by Jefferson, one unmistakably refers to bell pepper, seeds of which were sent from Mexico in 1824: "*Large Pepper,* a good salad the seeds being removed." Plantings of *Piperoni* in 1774 and *Capsicum Major* in 1812, among others, would seem to refer to bell pepper, as well.

Cayenne pepper (Capsicum frutescens L. var. *longum* Bailey) was planted by Jefferson as early as 1767. The presence of hot peppers in the West Indies

had been chronicled since 1494, according to Sturtevant.

Long pepper was a popular name for the elongated
cayenne, but it had been appropriated from the eastern *Piper longum,* the fruit spikelet of which had
fallen into disuse by the time of the voyages of discov-
ery.

The use of capsicum peppers seems to have come to
Virginia by way of the West Indies (see *Pepper Pot* and
Gumbo, for instance). The choice of pepper for *Pepper
Vinegar* is not altogether clear. I opt for cayenne because of the implied heat in comparing the flavor to
that of black pepper; also, Jefferson correspondence
in 1813 *(Garden Book)* refers to vinegar in which cayenne is steeped being used as seasoning. (This must
have been the basis for later southern barbecue mixtures.) However, some argue for the use of mild pepper
in this recipe, but I think that Mrs. Randolph would
have so specified. In any event, the use of hot peppers
in traditional Virginia cookery was highly skilled
and discreet, just enough to brighten the taste, not to
set it afire.

PEPPERPOT—Mrs. Randolph's recipe could be presented as a classically pure version of *Philadelphia
Pepper Pot,* of which apocryphal tales place the "in-
vention" during the War of Independence to feed a
hungry General Washington at Valley Forge. Pepper
pot was, however, a well-known dish from the British
West Indies, a great soup or stew the ingredients of
which were infinitely varied, and thickened or not

with cassareep (prepared cassava); its unvarying characteristic was the seasoning with cayenne pepper. *OED* cites Thomas Brown, about 1702: "That most delicate palate-scorching soop called pepperpot, a kind of devil's broth much eat in the West Indies." A century later, Mrs. Rundell gives a typical English interpretation that calls for mutton, pickled pork, mixed vegetables, lobster or crab, seasoned with "salt and Cayenne," and served with suet dumplings. But I believe that southern colonists had known the dish long before its appearance in cookbooks by way of black cooks.

PITCHCOCK—To *spitchcock* an eel is to prepare it for cooking, often spitting it down its length for roasting. *Pitchcock*, a corruption, was used by Mrs. Glasse in 1747, and *pitchcot* by Bradley in 1736. (To *spatchcock* a chicken is to pluck and cook it immediately on killing, an Irish usage, according to *OED;* no derivation is given for *spitchcock* but old recipes always specified that the eel be alive so that the idea of immediate cooking would seem to be common to both words.)

POTATOES—It is curious that the history of these common vegetables is so poorly understood; even highly regarded sources are contradictory, not to say self-contradictory. The white potato (*Solanum tuberosum,* related to tomato and eggplant) is native to the high valleys of the Andes, where it was long cultivated by the Incas. The sweet potato (*Ipomoea batatas,* not remotely related to either the white potato or true yam) is native to tropical America and is mentioned in 1494 as growing in Hispaniola by Chanca, physician to the fleet of Columbus, according to Sturtevant.

The confusion started when *potato,* from Haitian *batata (OED),* came to be applied not only to sweet potatoes but also to *papas,* an Inca name for white potato, thus hopelessly entangling their identities in early chronicles. Gerard in his *Herball* (1597) correctly identified them: sweets, already well known in England, he called simply *Potatoes,* saying that they grew in ". . . Spaine, and other hot regions," and that they "comfort, nourish, and strengthen the body, vehemently procuring bodily lust." White potatoes he called *Potatoes of Virginia,* explaining: "I have received roots hereof from Virginia . . . which grow & prosper in my garden," adding that the natives there called them *Pappus.* Fine drawings back up his identifications.

Sweet potatoes were imported from Spain. Already by 1586, Thomas Dawson had called for *Potaton* in a recipe *To make a tart that is a courage to man or woman,* referring to its putative aphrodisiac virtues. And they were sufficiently common for Shakespeare to have regaled his audiences with "Let the skye raine Potatoes" in *The Merry Wives of Windsor* with the same intent.

The white potato, at first shunned in Europe because it was thought to be poisonous, grudgingly came to be cultivated in Ireland early in the seventeenth century as food for the poor, thus accounting for its later popular name of Irish potato. Late in the century (see Forster in bibliography), the Royal Society helped to promote cultivation in England, but for nearly a century it remained food for the poor, typically eking out grain in bread, pastries, and puddings. (Mrs. Randolph gives such a recipe, no longer for the poor, for *Potato Paste (Appendix II)* and again for *Sweet Potato Buns* (see *breads*). Most English recipes calling for potatoes until around mid-eighteenth century are for *sweet* potatoes; rare exceptions are from reformers and enthusiasts.

The English settlers brought their prejudices with them and white potatoes were equally slow in being accepted in the Colonies for the most part. But in *Notes on the State of Virginia* (1782), Jefferson lists "Round potatoes. Solanum tuberosum" among plants that "were found in Virginia when first visited by the English; but it is not said whether of spontaneous growth, or by cultivation only. Most probably they were natives of more southern climates, and handed along the continent from one nation to another of the savages." And in *A Briefe and True Report of the New Found Land of Virginia* (1588) Thomas Hariot, a member of the Raleigh expedition, writes: "*Openauk* are a kind of roots of round forme of the bignes of walnuts, some far greater, . . . growing many together one by another in ropes, or as though they were fastnened with a string. Being boiled or sodden they are very good meate [food]." The identification of

Openauk with white potatoes is sometimes questioned, as is Gerard's provenance, so that Jefferson may also have been in error. But his notes prove that white potatoes had long been under cultivation in Virginia or he would not have accepted the premise.

In 1705, Beverley describes potatoes cultivated by the Indians, taking them to be the "*Spanish* Potatoes" of the herbals, adding: "I am sure, those call'd *English* or *Irish* Potatoes are nothing like these, either in Shape, Colour, or Taste," suggesting that he was not overly familiar with either. But Byrd, a naturalist and a contemporary, writes in 1737 that Virginians had long been cultivating "many species of potatoes," which might fairly be construed as including both sweets and whites. Both were regularly cultivated by Jefferson.

Jefferson felt very strongly about the depletion of the soil caused by growing maize and devised rational rotation plans involving corn, potatoes, and red clover, plans little heeded, alas.

POTATO PUMPKIN—I take this to be *calabaza* or West Indian pumpkin. In a letter to Samuel Vaughn, Jr., in 1790, Jefferson speaks of the *potatoe-pumpkin,* calling it thus "on account of the extreme resemblance of its taste to that of the sweet-potatoe," he says. He speculates that it "may be originally from your islands [Jamaica]." He adds that it "is well esteemed at our tables, and particularly valued by our negroes." (See *pumpkins and squash.*)

Sturtevant writes: "In 1884, there appeared in our

seedmen's catalogs, under the name of Tennessee Sweet Potato pumpkin, a variety very distinct, of medium size, pear-shape, little ribbed, creamy-white, striped with green, and the stem swollen and fleshy." (He says that it corresponds to "figures of a plant" given by Lobel in 1576 and 1591.) If this is the same plant, it demonstrates the lag between use and official notice, as well as the difficulties of historical identification.

PUDDINGS—On pudding procedure, I can do no better than to cite Hannah Glasse:

In boiled Puddings, take great Care the Bag or Cloth be very clean, not soapy, but dipped in hot Water and well floured. If a Bread-pudding, tie it loose; if a Batter-pudding, tie it close; and be sure the Water boils when you put the Pudding in, and you should move the Puddings in the Pot now and then, for fear they stick. When you make a Batter-pudding, first mix the Flour well with a little Milk, then put in the Ingredients by Degrees, and it will be smooth and not have Lumps; but for a plain Batter-pudding, the best way is to strain it through a coarse Hair Sieve, that it may neither have Lumps nor the Treadles of the Eggs: and for all other Puddings, strain the Eggs when they are beat. If you boil them in wooden Bowls, or China Dishes, butter the Inside before you put in your Batter; and for all baked Puddings, butter the Pan or Dish before the Pudding is put in. (*The Art of Cookery,* 1755.)

Note that a number of Mrs. Randolph's baked puddings are in crust, *Pumpkin Pudding* (facsimile), a most excellent recipe, and *Transparent Pudding (Ap-*

pendix II), for example. The latter recipe, differing only in language, is given by Mrs. Glasse in 1796 and is structurally identical to one given by Richard Bradley in 1736 for *Lemon Cheesecakes. From Mrs. M. N.* (being flavored with grated lemon rind, it is related to *lemon curd* and early lemon pies) and *Cheese-Cake Pudding,* contributed by *Mrs. Dr. P. C.* for Mrs. Tyree's *Housekeeping in Old Virginia.* Since archaic spellings of *cheese* often had but one *e,* we have the answer to the riddle of the name of that southern favorite *Chess Pie,* recipes for which vary no more from that for *Transparent Pudding* than those do among themselves; *Chess Cake* is also akin, if less directly. (The tradition of making cheesecake *without* cheese goes back to early seventeenth century and beyond; see *Martha Washington's Booke of Cookery.*) Basically the same syrupy buttery custard forms the base of southern pecan pie.

Baked puddings require a slow oven (300°F); if in a crust, start at 425°F and turn down after 15 minutes, or partially prebake the crust.

For the Indian puddings, reduce the amount of *cornmeal* or they will be too dense.

PUMPKIN and SQUASH—Both belong to the *Cucurbita* tribe, an exceedingly diverse and farflung group that includes cucumbers and melons, as well. Popular wisdom assigns uniquely American origin to pumpkins and squash, citing Algonquin *askutasquash* meaning that which is eaten green *(Webster),* and their cultivation by Indians, but botanists say that their origins are lost in time. (Effectively this means that any varieties found to be peculiar to a region have been cultivated by indigenous populations for a long time.) According to botanist Alex Hawkes, the ultimate home of *Cucurbita pepo,* which includes all summer crooknecks, zucchini, pattypan or cymling, and the ornamental gourds, as well as the pumpkin, may be the Himalayas. All winter squash are assigned to either *C. maxima,* certain forms of which were found growing alongside corn when Columbus came to our shores, or *C. moschata,* whose origins may have been in the Asiatic tropics, all according to Hawkes.

Various edible gourds had long been known in the Old World, perhaps for millennia. The *cucurbitas* (differentiated from *cucumeres,* cucumber, not always true in Greek sources) and *citrium* of Apicius of ancient Rome are variously translated by scholars into English as *marrows, pumpkin,* and *squash,* and into French as *courge* and *citrouille. The Forme of Cury* (about 1390) and *Le Ménagier de Paris* (about 1393) give recipes for *gourd* and *courge,* respectively. And Wyclif in his 1388 translation of the Bible speaks of "Gordis, and melouns" *(OED).* Precise varieties may be uncertain, but recipe instructions leave no doubt as to family characteristics.

Thomas Hariot, reporting on the Raleigh expedition of 1585, writes that Virginia Indians were cultivating: "*Macócqwer,* according to their severall formes called by us, *Pompions, Mellions,* and

Gourdes, because they are of the like formes as those kindes in England." In this regard, Thomas Johnson in an emendation to the 1636 edition of Gerard's *Herball* describes the "Virginian Macock or Pompion . . . *Pepo Virginianus*" as being "somewhat round, not extending in length, but flat like a bowle, but not so big as an ordinarie bowle, being seldome four inches broad and three inches long, of a blackish green colour when it is ripe. The substance or eatable part is of a yellowish white colour, containing in the middest a great deale of pulp or soft matter," going on to describe the seeds as being like those of "common Pompion, but smaller." (*Cucurbita maxima,* perhaps?)

It may be said that early writers were perfectly aware of the common family characteristics of members of the *Cucurbita* group.

ROCK FISH—Farther north along the coast, this fine fish is known as striped bass or striper—in some old books, *streaker.* (It has been naturalized along the American Pacific coast, according to Alan Davidson in *North Atlantic Seafood.*) It is closely related to the European sea bass, *bar, loup,* etc. William Wood, in *New Englands Prospect* (1634), praises it mightily, remarking the presence of "a bone in his head, which containes a sawcerfull of marrow sweet and good, pleasant to the pallat. . . . When there be great store of them, we onely eate the heads, and salt up the bodies for winter."

SALAMANDER—This implement is a long-handled iron plate that may be heated red-hot in order to brown food.

SALMAGUNDI—The dish appears in French by 1546 as *salmigondin* (from *sel,* salt, and *condire,* to season) according to *Robert;* but *OED* cites Blount in 1674, who describes *salmagundi* as being Italian and composed of "cold Turkey and other ingredients." Both may be right. Effectively, the dish is a composed salad using roasted fowl as central ingredient; recipes for it abound in eighteenth-century cookbooks.

SEA KALE—The bleached leaf stalks are the favored parts of this vegetable *(Crambe maritima),* but the shoots and the foliage, vaguely resembling kale, are also eaten. There are some nineteen entries concerning sea kale in Jefferson's *Garden Book.*

SHOTE—A shote (more properly *shoat*) is a young weaned pig; Mrs. Tyree in *Housekeeping in Old Virginia* (1879) specifies it as a pig between two and three months of age, and always cut into quarters. Mrs. Randolph gives five recipes for shote.

The term is from England, with a citation for *shote* by 1413 in *OED*.

SORREL—This delightful vegetable *(Rumex acetosa)* was highly popular in early Virginia; Jefferson grew it regularly, for example, and it was sold in the Washington markets (see *Appendix V).* It is now virtually impossible to find in most of the country. Another vegetable equally popular in Mrs. Randolph's day was *corn salad* (*mâche* in French) which was surely used by her in salads, although it is not mentioned. However, it was also grown by Jefferson and sold in the markets.

SOY—This is properly fermented soy bean sauce but in early American cookery, *soy* and *catsup* were not well differentiated, as seen in Mrs. Randolph's soy and catsup recipes for tomatoes. Just so, Richard Bradley gives a recipe in 1736 for a *Ketchup, in Paste. From Bencoulin in the East-Indies,* made of spiced strained beans.

SUGAR HOUSE SYRUP—This amber syrup "from the West Indies" recommended by Mrs. Randolph for preserving is, for all practical purposes, unavailable today. I understand that this was the original base for pecan pie and that modern versions are nothing like as good as the traditional one.

SYLLABUB—Traditional recipes call for agitating sweetened cream and milk, well laced with white wine or sherry (or ale or cider), until a great froth is obtained. The agitating is accomplished by methods varying from milking directly from the cow into a bowl of rich cream and wine to the use of a charming "syllabub churn," an ingenious device that produces a fine long-lasting froth. In addition to its other virtues, wine serves to lightly curdle the milk and "set" the fluffy mixture. This fortifying dessert drink was known by Tudor times and became enormously popular in colonial America. As ice cream became more available, the cool creamy syllabub came to be considered increasingly old-fashioned, although it did linger in the South (where it is now enjoying something of a revival).

Mrs. Randolph's recipe is not at all traditional and is quite beside the point.

TANSEY PUDDING—This dish harks back to the *Erbolat* of *The Forme of Cury* (about 1390), a baked omelet with many herbs, including tansey. A little later, the dish is called *tansye* and is cooked as a huge flat omelet. Tansey, the herb, has a strong aromatic scent and a bitter taste, and was associated with the bitter herbs of Passover, according to *OED*.

Mrs. Randolph's recipe is remarkably similar to that given in *Martha Washington's Booke of Cookery* (from about 1650), in that it calls for spinach, tansey, cream, sugar, spices, and bread crumbs, in addition to sorrel.

TIN DUTCH OVEN—This was an ingenious device for the purpose of roasting birds, which require a high roasting temperature. It was shaped like half a drum, lined with reflecting tin, and had a spit set in the axis. The combination of direct and reflected heat supplied the required temperatures. A hinged door on the rounded side away from the fire permitted easy tending of the bird, and a dripping pan set underneath caught the precious gravy. (See also *dutch oven*.)

TOMATO—The earliest recipe calling for tomatoes to have been published in America seems to be *To dress Haddock the Spanish Way,* given by Richard Briggs in 1792. It calls for "half a dozen love apples," to be stewed "very gently for half an hour." The recipe, lifted from Hannah Glasse, had been circulating in this country since 1765, perhaps earlier. (See also *catsup.*)

Jefferson included *tomatas* among usual garden stuffs in *Notes on the State of Virginia* (1782), and grew them regularly. They were sold in the Washington market from 1801 to 1809, appearing as early as July 16 and as late as November 17 (see *Appendix V*).

Helen Mendes, in *The African Heritage Cookbook* (1971), claims that blacks had long been cooking with tomatoes in Africa. If so, it would have been due to the Portuguese, who came to West Africa in the fifteenth century and had early and enthusiastically taken to the tomato. The tomato is native to tropical America; the very word derives from *tomatl,* its Nahuatl name *(Webster).* So that its introduction to Virginia could well have been part of the slave trade. Or it could have come by way of the West Indies. Or both. In any event, it was used much earlier and with more flair and abandon in the South than farther north where, to be sure, the climate was less hospitable.

Mrs. Randolph gives seventeen recipes calling for tomatoes (three of which appeared in 1825). Four of them are Spanish recipes; in many of the others, I suspect West Indian influence. Such richness and range of use indicate long familiarity with the tomato, illustrating once again the lag of the printed word behind usage. Yet, our leading food writers are able to state that no tomato recipes appeared in America until "the 1850's and '60's," and our most august newspaper solemnly declared recently that until a century ago, American recipes called for cooking tomatoes for at least three hours in order to dissipate the "poisons" they contained. I am unable to find any such recipes; indeed, Mrs. Randolph called for sliced, raw tomatoes in her recipe for Gazpácha (facsimile), and in 1839, Mrs. Bryan, in *The Kentucky Housewife,* suggested serving raw, sliced tomatoes seasoned with oil, salt, and pepper.

TURNIP ROOTED CABBAGE—This is almost surely rutabaga *(Brassica campestris, Napo-Brassica).* Jefferson notes in 1795 that "the leaf of the Ruta-bage resembles that of rape or cabbage & not at all that of turnep," and elsewhere refers to it as *Turnip Cabbage.* Hawkes reports that the British refer to it as *Turnip-Root Cabbage* today, as well as *Swedes.* And Mrs. Randolph's directions favor the rutabaga. Still, I must note that similar popular names have been used for *kohlrabi* by much later writers, Miss Parloa in 1887, for instance.

TURTLE, TO DRESS—This is a West Indian dish that seems to have come to the Colonies by way of English cookbooks. Richard Bradley, in *The Country Housewife and Lady's Director, Part II* (1736), gives recipes *"From a* Barbados *Lady"* for "Sea-Tortoise or Turtle [of] the West-Indies," whose fine flesh was "between that of Veal, and that of a Lobster," he says. He claims that the turtles weighed up to 200 pounds and were "frequently brought to *England* in Tubs of Sea Water, and will keep alive a long time." Hannah Glasse gives a recipe *To dress a Turtle, the West-India Way* in 1755 which is not so different from that of Mrs. Randolph; even Amelia Simmons gives one in 1796. Recipes varied, but cayenne seasoning was invariable. Turtle was expensive so *Mock Turtle Soup* was inevitable, but in fact, calf's head soups had long existed.

WEIGHTS AND MEASURES—The American habit of measuring all ingredients by the cup may be blamed on frontier life where scales were cumbersome but a cup was always to hand. But measuring flour by the cup is ludicrously inaccurate; a cup of the same flour may weigh from 3.7 to 6.3 oz. simply by varying the degree of tamping or sifting. In her bread recipe (facsimile), Mrs. Randolph states: "A quart of flour should weigh just one pound and a quarter," a moderately settled soft flour. Later writers were to specify four cups to the pound, very fluffy flour indeed, thus confounding flour measures ever since. And Fannie Farmer, the mythical inventor of accuracy in the kitchen, solemnly states in 1896: "2 cups flour (pastry) = 1 pound," a patent absurdity that was finally "corrected" to four cups in later editions. Most American flours, *normally settled,* weigh in at three cups to the pound, or thereabouts.

Mrs. Randolph's measures work out as follows:

1 lb. flour = 3¼ cups, scant
1 oz. flour = just over 3 tablespoons
1 cup flour = 5 oz. (141.75 grams)
1 tablespoon flour = 0.31 oz. (8.87 grams)

In addition, flours vary enormously in their absorptive powers. Southerners have historically used rather soft flour; to this day, blended "all-purpose" flour in southern states is softer (lower in gluten and less absorptive) than the same brand in northern states. In practical terms, northerners should scant flour measures or use softer flours when following southern recipes. (See also *flour.*)

Sugar, butter, and *lard* may all be regarded as amounting to 2 cups to the pound. *Butter the size of an egg* was understood to equal 2 oz., or 4 tablespoons.

Mrs. Randolph's volume measures correspond essentially to modern ones, or nearly. As late as Mary Lincoln, 1883, the teaspoon contained a *fluid dram,* a quarter-tablespoon; by 1896, Fannie Farmer says 3 teaspoons to a tablespoon. In the table below I am guided by Dr. Kitchener's *The Cook's Oracle* (Boston, 1822), where graduated pharmaceutical measures of glass are specified as being the most accurate.

1 *pint* = 16 fl. oz. (474 ml)
1 *cup* = 8 fl. oz. (237 ml)
1 *gill* = 4 fl. oz. (119 ml)
1 *wine glass* = 2 fl. oz. (60 ml)
1 large or *table spoon* = ½ fl. oz. (15 ml)
1 small or *tea spoon* = ⅛ fl. oz. (3.5 ml, a scant teaspoon)

The *dram* of the apothecaries weighs 60 grains or ⅛ oz. (In the avoirdupois system it equals 1/16 oz. but the substances involved were sold by pharmacists; also, Webster in 1806 gives only the ⅛ oz. definition.) The *scruple,* also an apothecaries' weight, equals 20 grains or ¹⁄₂₄ oz.

It will be seen that there were accurate measures long before Fannie Farmer, and indeed, long before Dr. Kitchener.

YEAST—Mrs. Randolph gives several ways to make yeast but finally proposes brewer's yeast for "those who can procure [it]." When working with period recipes, I normally find *a large spoonful of yeast* to be the equivalent of one-half ounce of fresh compressed yeast. However, skilled practitioner that she is, Mrs. Randolph dilutes the yeast to half-strength, thus using a small fraction of what modern American practice calls for. So that, particularly for the overnight sponge method in her bread recipe (facsimile), I propose but half that amount: *one-quarter ounce of fresh compressed yeast (or a level half-teaspoon of preservative-free dry yeast) for each quart (20 ounces) of flour* is more than ample. Shorter rising times, smaller batches, or enriched doughs may require a slightly higher proportion, but larger batches require a lower proportion. (The amount of dry yeast is not an error; everyone uses far too much yeast and with dry yeast, it is more serious. When working with dry yeast, I urge the use of the sponge method in all recipes; even 15 minutes does wonders in perking up the yeasts. Sugar in bread is not only unnecessary, it is an adulteration. (See also *flour* and *breads.*)

Please note that Mrs. Randolph does not heat the water, another sign of good practice. The yeasts take a bit longer to get started with water at room temperature but have healthier growth for it. Setting the dough where "it can have a moderate degree of warmth" is primarily a cautionary note for drafty winter days, I believe, and has little application in our overheated homes. Indeed, for the overnight method, a cool spot is more to the point.

Bibliography

In attempting to keep this bibliography within reasonable limits, I include only works to which I refer in my notes or which seem particularly pertinent to the subject at hand. Insofar as possible, I avoid listing undocumented or bowdlerized popular works dealing with the period (except where they purport to present major primary sources under discussion). Indeed, I list few secondary sources.

I had hoped to include a bibliography of cookbooks by Virginians, or published in Virginia, from 1742 to 1900, but it quickly became clear that it would be a monumental effort, quite beyond the scope of this work.

I list separately certain basic reference works referred to in my work so that they may quickly be located by the reader. Dates in parentheses refer to first editions unavailable to me. Material in brackets is information obtained otherwise than from the work itself.

I have deemed it useful to the reader to list modern reprints and facsimile editions where known to me. It is pertinent to note that works listed under Walter J. Johnson, Norwood, New Jersey, are published in conjunction with Theatrum Orbis Terrarum, Amsterdam.

K. H.

Basic Reference Works

Corominas, Joan. *Breve Diccionario Etimologico de la Lengua Castellana*. Madrid, 1961.

Halliwell, James Orchard. *Dictionary of Archaic and Provincial Words*. London, 1889. In facsimile, New York: Johnson Reprint, 1970.

Lowenstein, Eleanor. *Bibliography of American Cookbooks, 1742–1860*. Worcester, Massachusetts: American Antiquarian Society; New York: Corner Book Shop, 1972.

Oxford, Arnold Whitaker. *English Cookery Books to the Year 1850*. London: Oxford University Press, 1913.

Oxford English Dictionary (OED). London: Oxford University Press, 1971.

Robert, Paul. *Dictionnaire Alphabetique & Analogique de la Langue Française*. Paris: Societé du Nouveau Littré, 1967.

Vicaire, Georges. *Bibliographie Gastronomique*. Paris, 1890.

Webster, Noah. *A Compendious Dictionary of the English Language*. New Haven, 1806. In facsimile, New York: Crown, 1970.

Webster's New International Dictionary. Second edition. Springfield, Massachusetts, 1961.

Reading List

Acton, Eliza. *Modern Cookery for Private Families*. London: Longman, Brown, Green and Longmans (1845), 1855; the latter in facsimile, London: Elek, 1966. Same, *The whole revised and prepared for American housekeepers. By Mrs. Sarah J. Hale*. Philadelphia: 1845.
Miss Acton was a perceptive cook (heavily plagiarized by later writers) and is a good source for best English practice in the nineteenth century. The work saw a surprising nine editions in this country.

Apicius, The Roman Cookery Book. Translated from the Latin by Barbara Flower and Elisabeth Rosenbaum. London: Harrap, 1958.
This Latin-English pony version is useful.

Apicius, Les Dix Livres de Cuisine d'. Translated into French by Bertrand Guégan. Paris, 1933.
The voluminous scholarly annotations are invaluable. Apicius died about A.D. 30, so that this is the

earliest extant cookbook in the Western world. The work that we know, however, is not entirely classical as it was compiled in perhaps the fourth century, drawing on a number of Greek and Roman sources of various periods, and is preserved in several manuscripts, the earliest of which is from the ninth century. (The Vehling translation cannot be recommended for serious readers.)

Beverley, Robert. *The History and Present State of Virginia*. London: Richard Parker, 1705. Reprint, Chapel Hill: University of North Carolina Press, 1947.
Beverley was a historian and a perceptive observer. His chapters on foodstuffs in Virginia and on Indian agriculture and cookery are of particular interest here.

Bordley, J. B. *Essays and Notes on Husbandry and Rural Affairs*. Second edition. Philadelphia: Thomas Dobson, 1801.
Among recipes for pickling, ice cream, yeast, breads, etc., we find an interesting one for *Handy-Cake or Bread*, using pearl ash as leavening. The work is not listed by Lowenstein.

Bradley, Richard. *The Country Housewife and Lady's Director*. Sixth edition. London, 1736 (1727). Facsimile, with introduction by Caroline Davidson. London: Prospect Books, 1980.

Briggs, Richard. *The New Art of Cookery*. (London, 1788.) Philadelphia: Spotswood, Campbell, and Johnson, 1792; Boston, 1798; Philadelphia, 1798.

Bryan, Mrs. Lettice. *The Kentucky Housewife.* Cincinnati: Shepard & Stearns, 1839. Facsimile, Paducah, Kentucky: Collector Books, n.d. [c 1980]. This is an interesting cookbook, unjustly neglected. Lowenstein lists no edition prior to 1841, but *1839* is pristine in the facsimile.

Buckeye Cookery. Minneapolis, 1885 (1880). Reprint of 1883 edition, New York: Dover, 1975.
The recipes are contributed.

Byrd, William. *William Byrd's Natural History of Virginia or the Newly Discovered Eden.* (In German. Bern, 1737.) Reprint, including an English translation by Richard Croom Beatty and William J. Malloy. Richmond: Dietz Press, 1940. Byrd was a naturalist, member of the Royal Society, diarist, and founder of the city of Richmond.

Blot, Pierre. *Hand-Book of Practical Cookery.* New York: D. Appleton and Company, 1868 (copyright 1867). Facsimile of 1869 edition, New York: Arno, 1973.
This book by a French cook working in America is important and interesting.

Carolina Housewife. See Rutledge.

Carson, Jane. *Colonial Virginia Cookery.* Williamsburg: Wiliiamsburg Research Studies, 1968.
An invaluable study of the subject.

Carter, Susannah. *The Frugal Housewife, or Complete Woman Cook.* Boston, 1772; New York, 1792; Philadelphia, 1796, 1892, 1893.
All are editions of the English work; the last con-

tains "an appendix containing several new receipts adapted to the American mode of cooking." The fine plates are by Paul Revere. Reprint of first edition as *The Frugal Colonial Housewife;* New York: Dolphin, Doubleday, 1976. It is marred by inexplicable editing errors.

Child, Lydia Maria. *The American Frugal Housewife. Dedicated to Those Who Are Not Ashamed of Economy.* Boston, 1832 (1829). Facsimile; Columbus: Ohio State University Libraries, 1971.

Cornelius, Mary Hooker. *The Young Housekeeper's Friend.* Boston: Charles Tappan, 1846, 1871.

Cushing, Mrs. C. H., and Gray, Mrs. B. *The Kansas Home Cook-Book.* Fifth edition. Leavenworth, 1886.
The recipes are contributed.

Custis, George Washington Parke. *Recollections and Private Memoirs of Washington, by his Adopted Son.* New York, 1860.

David, Elizabeth. *English Bread and Yeast Cookery.* London, 1977. American edition with notes by Karen Hess. New York: Viking, 1980.
In order to understand the American loaf, it is necessary to understand the English loaf.
———*Spices, Salt and Aromatics in the English Kitchen: English Cooking, Ancient and Modern.* Harmondsworth: Penguin, 1970.
———*Summer Cooking.* Harmondsworth: Penguin, 1965.

————*Syllabubs and Fruit Fools*. Printed for the author, London, 1969. From the works of our foremost writer on food, I have chosen only those dealing primarily with English cookery.

Davidson, Alan. *North Atlantic Seafood*. New York: Viking, 1980.

A most important work.

Dawson, Thomas. *The Good Huswifes Jewell*. London, (1585?), 1586, 1596.

————*The Second Part of the Good Hus-wives Jewell*. (1585), 1587, 1596. Facsimile: Part I, 1596, and Part II, 1597, bound together. Norwood, N.J.: Walter J. Johnson, 1977.

Ebroïn Ary. *La Cuisine Créole*. Fort-de-France, Martinique: Émile Desormeaux, 1972.

Emerson, Lucy. *The New-England Cookery*. Montpelier: 1808.

The text is virtually a verbatim copy of *American Cookery*, Albany edition, by Amelia Simmons.

Eustis, Célestine. *Cooking in Old Créole Days*. New York: R. H. Russell, 1904, copyright 1903. Facsimile: New York: Arno Press, 1973 (of which the entire French language section of some 60 recipes and other material is excised without so much as noting it).

Evelyn, John. *Acetaria: A Discourse on Sallets*. London, 1699. Reprint: Brooklyn: Brooklyn Botanic Gardon, 1937.

A charming and enlightening work.

Farmer, Fannie Merrit. *The Boston Cooking-School Cook Book*. Boston: Little, Brown, 1896, 1914, 1916, 1926, 1965. Facsimile of first edition: New York: Crown, 1973.

The maiden aunt of home economists who marked the end of good American cookery.

Forme of Cury, The: A Roll of Ancient Cookery, compiled, about A. D. 1390 by the Master-Cooks of King Richard II . . . A Manuscript of the Editor of the same Age [1381] and Subject is Subjoined. Samuel Pegge, editor. London, 1780. *Forme of Cury* (pronounced *kewry*) may be translated as method of cookery. The two works are regarded as the earliest extant cookbooks in English.

Forster, John. *England's Happiness Increased, or A Sure and Easie Remedy against all succeeding Dear Years; By A Plantation of the Roots called* Potatoes, *whereof (with the Addition of Wheat Flower) excellent, good and wholesome Bread may be made . . . for halfe the Charge as formerly. . . . Invented and Published for the Good of the Poorer Sort.* London, 1664.

This rare work is a tract, backed by the Royal Society, effectively calling on Charles II to sponsor the cultivation of potatoes in England, specified by Forster as "*Irish Potatoes,* being little different from those of *Virginia*." They are carefully differentiated from sweet potatoes, "those of greatest request, [which] are the *Spanish Potatoes.*"

Benjamin Franklin on the Art of Eating together with

the Rules of Health and Long Life and the Rules to find out a fit Measure of Meat and Drink. With Several Recipes. With commentaries by Gilbert Chinard. Princeton: Princeton University Press for the American Philosophical Society, 1958.

    Texts from Franklin's writings concerning food.

Gerard, John. *The Herball or General Historie of Plantes. Gathered by John Gerarde of London, Master in Chirurgerie.* London, 1597. Facsimile: Norwood: Walter J. Johnson, 1973.

————Same, *Very much Enlarged and Amended by Thomas Johnson, Citizen and Apothecarye of London,* 1633, 1636. Facsimile of 1633 edition: New York: Dover, 1975. This was the first popular herbal in English to list a substantial number of New World plants so that it is precious. Fine drawings confirm his descriptions. In fact, the work was largely lifted from *Pemptades* by Rembert Dodoens as *Englished* from Dutch by a Dr. Priest; this does not dim the importance of the work.

[Glasse, Hannah]. *The Art of Cookery, Made Plain and Easy; Which far exceeds any Thing of the Kind ever yet published . . . By a Lady. Printed for the Author.* London, 1747.

————Same, by Mrs. Glasse, with additions and revisions. London, 1751, 1755, 1765, 1796 (listing only those editions I have consulted).

————Same, by Mrs. Glasse, *A New Edition.* Alexandria, Virginia: Cottom and Stewart, 1805, 1812.

Included are: *Several New Receipts Adapted to the American Mode of Cooking*. The work was the most important and popular work in the Colonies, as in England, during the latter half of the eighteenth century, with innumerable editions and revisions. The inventories at Mount Vernon show a copy of an early edition, I understand.

Graham, Sylvester. *A Treatise on Bread, and Bread-Making*. Boston: Light & Stearns, 1837. Facsimile, Milwaukee: Lee Foundation for Nutritional Research.

Hariot, Thomas. *A Briefe and True Report of the New Found Land in Virginia: of the commodities there found and to be raysed, as well marchantable, as other for victuall, building and other necessarie uses for those that are and shall be the planters there; and of the nature and manners of the naturall inhabitants*. London, 1588. Facsimile: Norwood: Walter J. Johnson, 1971.

Harrison, William. *The Description of England*. London, (1577, in *Holinshead's Chronicle I)* Reprint: F. J. Furnivall, editor. London: New Shakespeare Society, 1877.

Hartley, Dorothy. *Food in England*. London: MacDonald and Janes, 1954, 1975.

————*Lost Country Life* New York: Pantheon, 1979. There is much delightful material in these works, but do beware of her muddled dating; it has tripped many a "borrower."

Hawkes, Alex D. *A World of Vegetable Cookery.* New York: Simon and Schuster, 1968. Hawkes was a botanist, so that the work is useful in looking up modern scientific names and correlating them with common names. Curiously, his history of recent cultivation is unreliable; he places the introduction of broccoli in the United States in the 1920s, for instance.

[Hearn, Lafcadio]. *La Cuisine Creole.* New Orleans: F. F. Hansell & Bro., 1885. Facsimile: Louisville: Favorite Recipes Press, 1966.

Herman, Judith and Marguerite Shalett Herman. *The Cornucopia. Recipes, Containing Good Reading and Good Cookery from more than 500 years of Recipes, Food Lore, Etc.* . . . [1390–1899]. New York: Harper & Row, 1973.

The material from English and American sources is well chosen and makes a good read.

Hess, John L. and Karen Hess. *The Taste of America.* New York: Viking, 1977; Penguin, 1977.

A polemical and historical sketch of the decline of American food and cookery from colonial times to the junk and "gourmet" food of today.

Hess, Karen. *Martha Washington's Booke of Cookery and Booke of Sweetmeats; being a Family Manuscript, curiously copied by an unknown Hand sometime in the seventeenth century, which was in her Keeping from 1749, the time of her Marriage to Daniel Custis, to 1799, at which time she gave it to Eleanor Parke Custis, her granddaughter, on the occasion of her Marriage to Lawrence Lewis.* (Transcription, with Historical Notes and Copious Annotations.) New York: Columbia University Press, 1981.

Thomas Jefferson's Garden Book, 1766–1824. Edited by Edwin Morris Betts. Philadelphia: American Philosophical Society, 1944.
    A work of incalculable value, one that no student of American food can afford to be without. Its careful study would save many a red face.

Jefferson, Thomas. *Notes on the State of Virginia.* Paris (1784/85) [dated 1782 but written in 1781]; (1787), all according to Betts.
    The section concerning plants of Virginia is included in *Thomas Jefferson's Garden Book, 1766–1824.*

Kimball, Marie. *Thomas Jefferson's Cook Book.* Richmond: Garrett and Massie, 1949. Purportedly based on the *Martha Jefferson Randolph* collection.

——*The Martha Washington Cookbook.* New York: Coward-McCann, 1940. Purportedly based on the Washington MS. (see Hess).
    In both works, most of the recipes are bowdlerized beyond recognition.

[Kitchener, William]. *The Cook's Oracle . . . from the last London edition.* Boston: Munroe and Francis, 1822. Same, New York: J. & J. Harper, 1830.

Lea, Elizabeth E. *Domestic Cookery, Useful Receipts, and Hints to Young Housekeepers*. Baltimore: Cushings and Bailey, 1853 (1845).

Leslie, Miss [Eliza]. *Directions for Cookery; being a system of the art, in its various branches*. Philadelphia: E. L. Carey & A. Hart, 1837. Same, *Thirty-first Edition, with Improvements, Supplementary Receipts, and A New Index*. 1848. Facsimile of 1848 edition, New York: Arno, 1973.

————*The Indian Meal Book*. Philadelphia: Carey and Hart, 1847.

Miss Leslie was one of the great ladies of American cookery.

Lewis, Edna. *The Taste of Country Cooking*. New York: Alfred A. Knopf, 1976. The cookery of Freetown, Virginia (founded by freed slaves), as lovingly remembered by a descendant is evocative of Mrs. Randolph's cookery; the increase in sweetness is striking.

Lincoln, [Mary J.]. *Mrs. Lincoln's Boston Cook Book*. Boston: Roberts Brothers, 1883, 1893. Same; Little, Brown, 1926.

She was co-founder and first principal of the Boston Cooking School, of which this work was the first textbook, antedating Fannie Farmer's work by thirteen years.

Lucayos Cook Book, The: Being an Original Manuscript, 300 years old, never published. Found in the Bahamas. Kept . . . from A.D. 1660 to 1690 by a Noble Family of Elizabethan England. Nassau,

Bahamas, and Morrisburg, Ontario: Old Author's Farm, 1959.

Markham, G[ervase]. *The English Hus-wife, The inward and outward vertues which ought to be in a compleat woman. Printed at London for Roger Jackson, 1615.* (Second book of *Countrey Contentments.*) Facsimile: Norwood: Walter J. Johnson, 1973. Same, various formats and printers: 1623, 1631, 1637, 1660, 1683.

It was the most popular work of the seventeenth century and early came to the Colonies.

May, Robert. *The Accomplisht Cook.* London: Nath. Brooke, 1660, 1671, 1678.

An important work by a professional cook that early came to the Colonies.

Le Ménagier de Paris . . . composé vers 1393, par un bourgeois parisien. Introduction and notes by Jérôm Pichon. Paris, n.d. [1846]. Reprint: Luzarches, Daniel Morcrette, n.d. [about 1970].

Mendes, Helen. *The African Heritage Cookbook.* New York: Macmillan, 1971.

A serious discussion of black contributions to American cookery; the recipes do not come up to the quality of the text.

Morand, Simone. *Gastronomie Bretonne d'Hier et d'Aujourd'hui.* Paris: Flammarion, 1965.

Nègre, Dr. André. *Les Antilles á Travers Leur Cuisine.* Caen: Societé Guadaloupéen d'Editions, 1967.

Parloa, Maria. *Miss Parloa's Kitchen Companion.* Boston: Estes and Lauriat, 1887. One of the last perceptive American cookbook writers.

Parmentier, Antoine Augustin. *Le Parfait Boulanger.* Paris, 1778.

Penn Family Recipes. Cooking Recipes of Wm. Penn's Wife, Gulielma. Edited by Evelyn Abraham Benson. York: George Shumway, 1966.

The fair copy is dated 1701 but the recipes are from mid-seventeenth century, or earlier. It is in the keeping of the Historical Society of Pennsylvania.

The Picayune's Creole Cook Book. New Orleans: *The Picayune,* (1900), 1901. Facsimile, 1901 edition: New York: Dover, 1971.

Porter, Mrs. M. E. (Prince George Court-House, Virginia). *Mrs. Porter's New Southern Cookery Book.* Philadelphia: John E. Potter, 1871. Facsimile: New York: Arno, 1973.

Price, Rebecca. *The Compleat Cook.* Edited by Madeleine Masson. London: Routledge & Kegan Paul, 1974.

"This Booke was written by me: Rebecca Price in the Yare 1681." It continues to her death in 1740. The recipes are of great interest but are not arranged chronologically.

Raffald, Elizabeth. *The Experienced English Housekeeper.* London, (1769), 1789. Same, Philadelphia: Dobson, 1801; Webster, 1818.

[Randolph, John, Jr.]. *A Treatise on Gardening by a Citizen of Virginia* [Williamsburg]. Richmond, (c. 1706–65, 1793). Reprint, edited by Marjorie F. Warner. Richmond, 1924. This seems to have been the earliest gardening manual published in Virginia. The 1793 edition was in Jefferson's library, according to Betts.

Randolph, Martha Jefferson Recipe Manuscript Collection, early recipes in the hand of Virginia Trist, her daughter. Alderman Library, University of Virginia.

These voluminous papers document upper class Virginia cookery from the days of Monticello and the White House (with recipes of Le Maire) down through the nineteenth century (with recipes as late as 1895). The decline in quality is striking. This national legacy is available to us only in ludicrously bowdlerized form (see Kimball).

Rorer, Mrs. S. T. *Mrs. Rorer's Philadelphia Cook Book*. Philadelphia: Arnold and Company, 1886.

[Rundell, Mrs. Maria Eliza]. *A New System of Domestic Cookery, formed upon principles of economy, and adapted to the use of private families. By a lady*. First American edition, Boston: William Andrews, 1807. Second edition, Boston, Philadelphia, Richmond:1807. Same, New York: 1814, 1817.

A highly influential work in both North and South in the first quarter of the century.

[Rutledge, Sarah]. *The Carolina Housewife, or House and Home: by a Lady of Charleston*. Charleston: W.

R. Babcock & Co., 1847. Facsimile, *With an Intro-duction and Preliminary Checklist of South Car-olina Cookbooks Published before 1935, by Anna Wells Rutledge*. Columbia: University of South Carolina Press, 1979.

This work is of rare importance and has pre-viously been neglected. The introduction by an-other charming "Lady of Charleston" who speaks of "Cousin Sally" is delightful and illuminating.

Salaman, Redcliffe. *History and Social Influence of the Potato*. Cambridge: Cambridge University Press, 1946.

Simmons, Amelia. *American Cookery, or the art of dressing viands, fish, poultry and vegetables, and the best modes of making pastes, puffs, pies, tarts, puddings custards and preserves, and all kinds of cakes, from the imperial plumb to plain cake. Adapted to this country, and all grades of life. By Amelia Simmons, an American orphan*. Hartford: Hudson & Goodwin, 1796. Facsimile, with intro-duction by Mary Tolford Wilson, New York: Oxford University Press, 1958. Albany: Charles R. and George Webster, 1796, second edition.

Smith E[liza?]. *The Compleat Housewife; or, Accom-plish'd Gentlewoman's Companion: being a Collec-tion of upward* of Five Hundred of the most approved Receipts in Cookery, Pastry, Confection-ary, Preserving, Pickles, Cakes, Creams, Jellies, Made Wines, Cordials . . . fit either for private families, or such publick-spirited gentlewomen as would be beneficent to their poor Neighbors. Williamsburg: William Parks, 1742.

Smith, John, Captain. *A Map of Virginia, with a Description of the Countrey*. London, 1612.

————*The Generall Historie of Virginia, New-England and the Summer Isles*. London, 1624.

Sturtevant, Edward Lewis. *Sturtevant's Notes on Edible Plants*. Edited by U. P Hedrick. Albany: J. B. Lyon, State of New York, Agriculture Department, 1919. Reprint, as *Sturtevant's Edible Plants of the World*. New York: Dover, 1972. The work lay in manuscript for more than thirty years, making it now nearly a century old, so had neither the benefit of recent botanical research on origins of plants and reclassifications, nor the present advantage of easy access to Jefferson's *Garden Book* and related papers. Nevertheless, it remains one of the more solid works on the subject and, above all, is relatively easy of comprehension by those of us not trained in botany. His bibliographical references are perticularly useful.

Turner, William. *The Names of Herbes in Greke, Latin, Englishe, Duche, Frenche with the Commone Names Herbaries and Apotecaries Use*. London, 1548. Reprint, edited by James Britten, London: English Dialect Society, 1881.

This is an extremely useful edition because the names are correlated with nineteenth-century scientific names.

[Tusser, Thomas]. *A Hundreth Good Pointes of Husbandrie*. London, 1557. Facsimile, Norwood: Walter J. Johnson, 1973.

Tyree, Marion Cabell. *Housekeeping in Old Virginia*. Louisville: John P. Morton, 1879. Reprint, Louisville: Favorite Recipes Press, 1965.

Mrs. Tyree was the compiler of this collection of contributed recipes; nearly 250 contributors are listed, among them Virginia's first names. As such, the work may be considered to fairly represent upper-class Virginia cookery of the period.

Virginia Cookery, Past and Present. Including A Manuscript Cook Book of the Lee and Washington Families. Franconia, Virginia: The Woman's Auxiliary of Olivet Episcopal Church, 1957, 1970.

The manuscript (now in the keeping of Arlington House) was started by Elizabeth Collins Lee (Mrs. Richard Bland Lee) who was born in 1761. *The Washington attribution is in error;* it is based on a single recipe signed *Martha,* a practice which would have been highly disrespectful towards an older woman of station. (In fact, only servants were attributed thus in these manuscripts and it is invariable in my experience.) The recipes are dated as late as 1880, and are of great interest. The bulk of the work comprises contributed recipes and as such reflects the state of Virginia cookery today fairly accurately, although there is a conscious effort on the part of many contributors to give heirloom recipes. There are also occasional recipes gleaned from old Virginia cookbooks, so that the work is a useful one.

Martha Washington's Booke of Cookery. The manuscript is in the keeping of the Historical Society of Pennsylvania. [See Hess.)

[Webster, Mrs. A. L.]. *The Improved Housewife, or Book of Receipts . . . By A Married Lady.* Hartford, (1844), 1845; the latter in facsimile, New York: Arno, 1973.

Whistler's Mother's Cook Book. Edited by Margaret MacDonald. New York: G. P. Putnam's Sons, 1979.

    The manuscript was started in 1821 by the first wife of James McNeill Whistler's father and continued by his second wife, the mother portrayed by the artist. The recipes are altogether typical of American home manuscripts of the day. I regret to say that they are not arranged chronologically.

White, Florence. *Good Things in England.* London: Jonathan Cape, 1932, 1968.

Wightman, S. C. Cookery manuscript. New England, most likely Connecticut. Dated May 1824. In author's possession.

Wilson, C. Anne. *Food and Drink in Britain. From the Stone Age to Recent Times.* London: Constable, 1973; Harmondsworth: Penguin, 1976.

    A valuable reference.

Wood, William. *New Englands Prospect. A true, lively, and experimental description of that part of* America, *commonly called New England: discovering the state of that Countrie, both as it stands to our new-come* English *Planters; and to the old Native Inhab-itants.* London, 1634.

THE INDEX

Mrs. Randolph had a way of referring to recipes by other than their given names. Such titles, as well as those of other "lost" recipes and occasional explanatory material, are given in brackets. All titles are given in capital letters, followed immediately by page number. Particularly pertinent references to principal product or to the history of the recipe are given in bold face.